MULK RAJ ANAND
THE NOVEL OF COMMITMENT

MULK RAJ ANAND
THE NOVEL OF COMMITMENT

S.A. KHAN

ATLANTIC PUBLISHERS AND DISTRIBUTORS

Published by
ATLANTIC PUBLISHERS AND DISTRIBUTORS
B-2, Vishal Enclave, Opp. Rajouri Garden, New Delhi-27
Phones : 5413460, 5429987

Sales Office
4215/1, Ansari Road, Darya Ganj, New Delhi-02
Phones : 3273880, 3285873, 3280451
Fax : 91-11-3285873
e-mail : info@atlanticbooks.com
web : www.atlanticbooks.com

ISBN 81-7156-958-7

Typeset at
APD Computer Graphics, Delhi

Printed in India at
Mehra Offset Press, Delhi

Dedicated to

PROF. KHAN ANSAR S.
KHAN SHOEB S.
SARIBA FATIMA S.
and
KHAN IMTIYAZ S.

FOREWORD

Mulk Raj Anand is one of the few Indian English Writers internationally acclaimed as a novelist though his works include short stories, criticism, fairy tales, autobiography, language, history, education, politics, arts, films, folk theatres, dance, music feminism and contemporary Indian culture. This could be possible for Anand as once another eminent Indian writer emphasised in an interview. "I think we have an advantage over all other countries in the world where life is so standardised that they are hard up for material. We have abundance in the work of Anand on the rigidity of caste system, the tyranny of class-system, religious bigotry and the predicament of women as one does in the works of a contemporary, Munshi Prem Chand.

Anand too like many others was profoundly influenced by Karl Marx, the founder of Communism. Marx gave a call to action to workers of all countries to unite against the exploitation of the working classes by the Capitalists. In India, the exploitation is in varied and multiple forms and is almost endless. Anand, therefore, could write so much about exploitation including all-sided by the alien Rulers. Marxism was acceptable to Anand perhaps because it was scientific and rational and though there is sufficient impact of Western education, no where Anand forgets his being an Indian-Hindu-Kshatriya.

Certainly to write about Anand, his life and work with a critical approach is no easy task, nay a maiden scholar may be lost even in the midway. The author therefore has preferred to avoid to stake any tall claim and in all sincerity has admitted his work to be a modest attempt to limn out the Marxist orientations as embedded in novels of Anand, vividly presenting Marxian ideology which becomes the essential component of Anand's fictional corpus and in fact this study attempts to point out the exact area of Anand's strength by casting a flood of light on the hitherto unexplored area of critical exposition. The author has undoubtedly succeeded in this task.

What has attracted my attention most while going through the book are references to the Allama Mashriq Dr. Mohammed Iqbal, though there is no direct clue to know what fascinated Dr. Iqbal to advise Anand to leave for England for higher education and even to financially help him, was it Punjab or something else. The rare affection coupled with advice of Dr. Iqbal speaks itself of their intimate relationship, "If the s*elf* is living then the Ocean is limitless. Go son conquer the world", reciprocally the gratitude is expressed by Anand in these words "And I felt exalted that this sage, this poet and philosopher was giving me advice. He seemed me more than my father, who had generated me." Anand frankly wrote to his father. "And I saw the contrast of affection given to me by Dr. Iqbal."

"Iqbal is our teacher" Anand observes in his conversation with T.S. Eliot and a step further he rejects his father's intermittent admonitions and wants very much to follow the advice of Dr. Iqbal. Anand at one stage ventured to *shape* himself into Dr. Iqbal's individual of the long poem "The Secret of Self", to become "a hero, a man of 'Will' and action — a god" but under the spell of Hindu religion a making of an individual is different. Dr. Iqbal observes that *The Holy Quran* contains much wisdom about self, in his poem "The Secret of Self" ("Israr") therefore he has asked for the growth of man, of the individual and thus the diversity of paths.

The book is be a valuable addition to the World of Literary Criticism and of immense utility to those who want to further explore the areas of critical exposition of Anand's life and works.

K. MANZURUDDIN

PREFACE

The present book makes a modest attempt to limn out the Marxist-orientations as embedded in the novels of Mulk Raj Anand. Anand is often described as a "committed" writer, though he does not want to be aligned with writers committed to a set of ideologies. He prefers to call himself a humanist, and many of the critics in the past have endeavoured to place him in the European Hellenistic tradition. Most of them, it appears, have relied on the critical pronouncements of Mulk Raj Anand which he made from time to time. But, I feel, that a study of Mulk Raj Anand is not complete unless his work is fixed in the context of left-wing writers, both continental and European. The book underscores this particular aspect, and vividly presents Marxian ideology which becomes the essential component of Anand's fictional corpus. Right from the beginning, Anand has been working towards this fixed goal of establishing a rapport between his conceptions and their actualizations, between man and society, and has always been dreaming of a millennium of happiness. Since the main thrust of the thesis is on Marxist-orientations, the other ancillary fictional modes such as the narrative techniques, the linguistic virtuosity which have largely gone into shaping of his novels, are deliberately left out. In fact, the book attempts to pinpoint the exact area of Anand's strength, by casting a flood of light on the hitherto unexplored or partially explored areas of critical exposition.

I am indebted to my research guide, Dr. K.R. Rao, who has helped me through a number of unresolvable critical antinomies. He has lent his much time for probing discussions. I am also thankful to Dr. Mulk Raj Anand who has clarified some of the moot points by writing personal letters to me. I am also thankful to Principal M.R. Baig who has evinced a particular interest in the progress of my research work.

My thanks are also due to Mr. M.K.R. Naidu of S.N.D.T. Women's University, Mumbai and Mr. S.K. Markad, Librarian of my college for their kind co-operation in lending the books which I needed most.

S.A. KHAN

CONTENTS

1

Into the Smithy

Of all the Indo-Anglian novelists, Mulk Raj Anand is the most prolific and the most committed writer and belongs to, what Prof. K.R.S. Iyengar calls "the Great Tradition", alongwith the other two elderly novelists like R.K. Narayan and Raja Rao. Anand's career as a novelist could be properly evaluated and assessed only when his life-story is reconstructed, for his life and work coalesce and intermingle at every stage of his development as an artist. His is an uneventful life marked by a commixure of unstinted joy and abysmal frustrations by enlivened all the more by the parental tutelage and the comforts he has had in the idyllic surroudings of his home-town in Punjab. In fact, Anand, the Man and Anand, the Novelist remain inseparable, for his life is one long story of an individual coming to terms with life and art. As Anand observes :

> ...the criticism of my novels would have to be by internal evidence of the novels themselves...the autobiographical novels become very important as sources indicative of energies let loose in my young life.... The connection between my life and my writings is more intimate than in other novelists. I write as I live. My life is my message. My past is my future.[1]

Anand shares with many of his contemporaries, his expressive concerns and his humanist sympathies; but what differentiates him from other novelists of his time is his fiery commitment to left-wing ideas which seems to have broadened his global understanding of life. One can understand his penchant for, and commitment to, doctrinnaire principles as imbeded in, what he calls, 'comprehensive historical humanism'. He explores its different nuances and ramifications of perspectives both in the individual and collective fate of the Indian masses, burdened as they are under continual processes of near denudation and ossification. Anand's proletarian humanism aligns him with such literary luminaries as Zola and Balzac, Spender and Isherhood, Farrell and Wright, Tolstoy and Dostoevsky, Yashpal and Premchand, Iqbal and Bhai Veer Singh, Gandhi and Nehru, and other doctrinnaire utopians like Karl Marx and Lenin. These eminent men of letters and political connoisseurs have provided him so much of ideological fulcrum that Anand becomes a 'committed' writer not by sheer accident, but by conscious choice. Thus the evolution of Anand from a mere social chronicler to a 'committed' humanist is attempted in the succeeding pages of this chapter such that a coherent vision of his ideological commitments and his flair for "so many freedoms"* could be consistently limned out.

Anand has written in his *Apology for Heroism*** ... "Any writer, who said that he was not interested in *la condition humaine,* is either posing or yielding to a fanatical love of isolation — a perverse and clever defence of the adolescent desire to be different."[2] He feels that "a writer must go straight to the heart of the problem of our time, the problem of human sensibility in present complex world, the tragedy of moral man."[3] He neither shies away from his ideological commitments nor does he feel ashamed of using fiction for all his propagandistic purposes. So committed is he to his creed that Anand endeavours to apotheosise man and tries to bring amelioration to the millions of hapless Indian masses subjected to the worst forms of social indignity, apathy, boredom and ugliness. He endeavours to restore to the India's 'lost generation' of untouchables, of coolies, and of indentured labourers both human dignity and decency, which were perforce denied to them by a congeries of social and historical forces. Anand views literature as

---

* The slogan of Russian Revolution was to free mankind from all kinds of slavery. In his speech on 8th November, 1907 Lenin exhorted.

"We shall free mankind from the slavery of man."

** It is worth pointing that it was published in 1943, in the form of a long essay entitled *In Search of Faith.*

a religious and philosophical art, with his comprehensive and integrating principle of historical humanism forming the *weltanshauung* of his fictional corpus. Anand's sojourn to England and his undertaking of philosophical research under the guidance of Prof. Hicks have further broadened his intellectual perceptions and his concern for the humanity. Fortunately for Anand, he comes under the influence of Marxian ideology, and with a typical Bloomsbury intellectual's dexterity and agglutinative temper, Anand endeavours to synthesise both Western and Eastern art forms in his fiction.

Anand's impressionable years are in the nature of continual assimilation and ingression, his mother's broad-based humanism and his father's rationalist temper tending to make his attitude to life a whit confused but not totally ambivalent. His father dreampt of his son becoming the member of Indian Civil Service, which was considered a prestigious job in those days. There were only two options left for Anand either to opt for the Indian Civil Service or go in for teaching, as a substitute for bureaucratic job. To escape from his father's fussy but benevolent regimen and the prospect of joining the government job, as he describes factotumic, Anand came to England to study philosophy and came under the influence of left-wing ideology in which he found the prospect of security not only for himself but for the collective Indian masses. He even spearheaded Marxian Movement in Indian Literature by founding 'All India Progressive Writers Association' with other Indian writers committed to the same cause of the Indian 'have-nots'. The ideological commitment seems to have given Anand the figure of authority and purposive direction which he has lost at home, as an adolescent. He has accepted, not without any reason the Western scientific and technological achievements, but found Western capitalism, which was beginning to spread its nefarous tentacles, as uncompromising. Thus, Anand's proletarian bias is the result of his avid reading of Karl Marx and the conceptual and ideological influences of humanists like M.N. Roy, Gandhi and Nehru, and Western philosophers like Hume, Locke, Hegel and Kant, who seem to have whetted his intellectual curiosity and changed the whole perspectives of life. Anand, as all reformists, inveigles against all forms of caste, creed and wealth, which he feels, are a bane of the

Indian society, and he develops a genuine compassion for the underprivileged. He resents all forms of social repression and superstition, orthodoxy and regimentation to reinforce the inviolable truth that 'Man is the measure of all things.'*

Anand's unswerving faith in the concept of 'the whole man', coupled with his proclivity for a proletarian revolutionary idealism, gets further reinforcement as he plunges into the maelstrom of Indian politics, albeit consciously. As he observes :

> ... the artist knows how to choose and select the centre of his attack, ...there is a living myth and a dead myth, which is the basis of revolutionary romanticism, must be really creative and must help men to integrate in society and...the function of art in society approximates to the real needs of people in our time, then the artist is a revolutionary in the true sense...the way to a new life, the artist stands as an inspiring force...reconstructing the future society out of the shambles of a near prehistoric present.
>
> Capitalism based on the idea of private property, the exploitation of labour for profit and competitive national interests, failed to stabilize itself and to solve its inherent crises, except through fascism and war, the hold of this system and its ancillary ideas and institutions on the minds of a great portion of the world still persists. So that a fraudulent use of the word 'Democracy' is made to cover all the defaults of reaction. Thus, one of the first things to be done in the modern world is to educate the people, to place the vast researches accumulation of knowledge collected in the researches of the past at the disposal of everyone,

---

* M.N. Roy in his book entitled *New Humanism : A Manifesto,* says : "Man is the measure of all things (Protagoras) or Man is the root of mankind." (Marx)

M.N. Roy, *New Humanism* : *A Manifesto*, Ajanta Publications, Delhi (1981), p. 62.

> so that man can thereby learn to recognize the fundamental principles of human living and exercise vigilance in regard to the real enemies of freedom and socialism.[4]

While Anand concedes his inspirational fiat to the historical humanism, his preoccupation with the concept of 'the whole man' seems to emanate from his comprehensive understanding of the social *milieu* around him. Anand places human being at the apex of creation and freely admits that he has been working under the influence of European Hellenism. With an unflagging faith in the perfectability of man from Hobbesian 'noble savage' to the enlightened messiah — that seems to be the recurring pattern in most of Anand's novels. He observes elsewhere, 'man excels in his creative imagination, in his capacity to transform himself, in the energy with which he can raise himself to tremendous heights of dignity and redeem the world from its misery and pain'.[5]

Thus, Anand's development as a novelist is *pari passu* with his avowal of historical humanism both as an artistic credo and as an all-embracing religion; he has merely found for his felt-experiences a verisimilitude via his fictional experimentations. Anand feels the urgency and the immediacy of communicating all these social impulses which seem to have provided him with an opportunity for emotional cleansing and an ambience to work with. Anand the writer, and Anand the man, remain an enigma, though one can read much between lines in his critical pronouncements. He is passionately concerned with the inarticulate Indian men and women and the atrocities perpetrated on them by the complicity of social and economical orders, which, in fact, constitute the cause for his vociferous protestations. He 'writes in an angry reformist way, like a less humorous Dickens of the personal suffering induced by moribund social values', and touchingly speaks of the miseries of the countless Indian untouchables, coolies and dentured labourers. As Prof. K.R.S. Iyengar points out :

> Thus, when Anand started writing fiction, he decided he would prefer the familiar to the fancied, that he would avoid the highways of romance and sophistification but explore the bylanes of the outcastes and the peasants, the sepoys, and the

> working people. It was, however, no laborious exercise of self-conscious proletarianism. To Anand it was merely the easier and more natural way; he was himself of the proletariat.... It is the atmosphere of the late twenties and the early thirties, the air was filled with the dust of politics and infected with the fumes of man's inhumanity to man, but it was not altogether unrelieved by hope.... It is also worthy of mention that Anand is a 'committed wirter'.[6]

Though Anand does not concede that he is a diehard Marxist, with all its ancillary modes of social radicalism, his championing of the cause of the underprivileged is not without a deep-seated rationale. When 'his imagination burns and the dross of propaganda is consumed, Anand becomes a novelist of considerable power'. He feels that he is truly a humanist, spearheading the cause of the poor and the lowly, the oppressed and the depraved. He does not believe in any institutionalized religion nor in Godhood, in the abstract metaphysical terms. Like Tolstoy, whom he considers his mentor, he comes very nearly into accepting the secular religion and takes an interesting cue, for all the creedal preoccupations, from the Western humanist tradition. Anand decidedly belongs to the tradition of the nineteenth century writers, and writes under the preponderant influence of the European hellenistic tradition, particularly that of the French and of the Russian; and the writers whom he overtly or covertly wooes are Tolstoy, Flaubert, Zola and Balzac. He himself admits rather candidly that he carries with him the double burden on his shoulders "the Alps of European tradition and the Himalayas of the Indian past".[7]

Anand is as much concerned with the decadent aspects of the Indian tradition as he is with the upholding of the finer elements in the Indian social life. In this respect, he comes closer to the nineteenth century fictionalist like Hardy than anybody else, especially in his portrayal of the decadence of the Indian rural life. Anand's pessimism, Faulknerian in its import and intensity, finds a remarkable crystallisation in most of his early fictional experimentations; but they are not altogether devoid of the radiant hope, as indicated in his early novels. But somehow, a streak of pessimism underscores and ordinates the whole corpus of his fiction though Anand comes out with a timely apology to say that he is not as stark a pessimist as Hardy has been.

Anand's commitment to his social creed and his obsessive preoccupation with the underdogs could be well elucidated *inter alia* his fictional experimentations. His sociological predilections, which are implicated even in his first novel written as early as 1935, are in themselves the product of all these confluence of social and historical influences which seem to have provided him with a definitive impetus for his future forays into the human predicament, more particularly the seamier side of the Indian social life. Anand observes elsewhere : "The problem I tried to face as a writer was strictly a private, but a private-public problem."[8] In his own search for identity and self-differentiation, and in his earnest zeal to apprehend the manifoldness of life, he is entangled not merely in finding a solution to his personal, but collective problems as well. Anand is interested in the need for "Revolution" and "togetherness" and a new "sense of community" as the principles of this humanistic religion and writes fiction with an inner compulsion in order to ameliorate the lot of the common men so that they might come out of their pre-destined predicament of the trauma of self-isolation. So passional is Anand's commitment to left-wing ideology that he undoubtedly uses it in the service of his propaganda.* The biographical details are summarised here with a view to limning out Anand's transition from confused individualism to a broad-based historical humanism, a fact which was true with the other Indian revolutionary intellectuals writing between 1914 and 1947. His life-

---

* In a personal letter to me, Anand has made this observations :

The word 'commitment' is an "English term used somewhat derisively against writers of the Left, who are supposed to be 'social realists', stooges of Soviet Union. I feel it does not apply to our Indian writers, Prem Chand, Sarat Chatterji or Takazi Shiv Shankar Pillai. Our writers are from within Indian languages where there are no critical categories, like naturalism, realism, idealism are applicable.

To understand my evolution as a writer...read my autobiographical novels, which were written before the published novels, *Untouchable, Coolie* and the confessionals reveal my conversion from innocence to experience of pain. I began to understand the roots of misery around me before I began to write novels. And those novels are not of 'commitment' but of protest, on all plans and arising from my human concerns. (Anand's letter to me dt. 11-2-1986)

story will also help one to understand the type of an intellectual he is and, the formative influences which have gone into the shaping of his 'emotional and intellectual make-up'.

Mulk Raj Anand was born on December 12, 1905, in North India, in an undivided Hindu family of Kshatriyas, who were traditional coppersmiths. He is the third among five sons of Lal Chand who served as a head-clerk in the British Indian Army. His mother Ishwar Kaur, was a Sikh from the sturdy peasant stock, steeped as she was in orthodoxy and conservatism, and from whom Anand seemed to have developed a flair for reading the ancient Indian epics and mythological lores. Anand spent his formative years in two cantonments, Mian Mir and Nowshera; on his mother's village of Daska near Gujranwalla in Punjab and in his father's home-town of Amritsar. His father, Lal Chand, though apparently compassionate, was an astute disciplinarian. Anand was admitted into a British Indian School because it was considered, by the middle class parents, to offer good education. In 1914 his father became a member of Arya Samaj, a reformist Hindu organisation. Anand detested his father's "hotch-potch" world of which "he early began to perceive inconsistencies"[9] and he never spared his father for "paying lip service to the tenets of Hinduism while... (seeking) to amass a fortune through sufficient service as well through various sidelines in money-lending, buying and selling houses, accepting mortgages of property and bribes".[10] He rejected his father's mode of life which in fact meant to him a rejection of the tensions and disbalances which he saw in himself and in his environment. Though he considered his father to be a hero in his precocious, adolescent days, he later seemed to have developed a negative attitude to life. There were occasions when he was beaten up and had to undergo a cascade of abuses and reprimands unleashed by his father which aroused in him a feeling of resentment and revolt. Anand has observed :

> I remember the first time I was beaten by father. I had stolen a rich, luscious mango... it may be that the violent thrashing which I received then made me hate him (Lal Chand) forever on one side of my nature and largely transformed me into the uncompromising rebel that I became, gave the

> spoilt self-willed child in me the impetus of an overdeveloped sense of grievance and misery.[11]

Anand was nine years old when the First World War broke out, when the family shifted to Amritsar; he lived there from 1914 to 1925. During this period Kausalya, his cousin died in 1916 an incident which emotionally perturbed Anand. Anand's passage into adult life constitutes yet another chapter in his evolution as a man and as a creative artist.

Anand joined Khalsa College in Amritsar which provided him an opportunity to come out into the open from the claustrophobic home environment. For brief spell, he took part in the Indian struggle for Freedom which was strongly resented to by his father. During the college days, he fell in love with a Muslim girl, who was the sister-in-law of his college friend, Mohammed Nur. Anand very much wanted to marry her, but was prevented timely though, by his orthodox family members who disapproved of his unconventional marriage with a Muslim girl. Anand considered this a personal affront, and when the girl committed suicide in desperation, he was rudely shocked and felt guilty. During his college days, Anand frequently made trips to Lahore to visit the famous philosopher-poet, Dr. Mohammed Iqbal, whom he claimed as his paragon. After graduating with honours in 1925, and at the behest of Dr. Mohammed Iqbal, Anand prepared himself to go to London for higher studies, with the financial assistance provided by Dr. Iqbal and Lal Mohan, the Principal of his college and his mother. He felt that his continual stay in India would hamper his growth and it would also mean acceptance of his father's dictatorial regiment which was uncompromising to him; his "search for truth would have been lost in the search for position."[12] After a virtual emotional break and disjunction from the patriarchal authoritarianism, Anand left for England in search of a foothold and an ideology that best suited his intellectual nourishment. Anand's philosophical research did not take him afar though and the thoughts of John Locke, George Berkeley, David Hume and Bertrand Russell seemed as elusive and intractable to him as they had been in the past. He could not cope with the rigours of this intellectual exercise and was baffled by the complexities and subtleties of the Hegelian dialectics. On Professor Hick's behest, he left for a small village near London, and started reading avidly Adamson's *The Development of Modern Philosophy*. There, he came in contact with Irene, the daughter of a Welsh Professor, whose contact paid him abundantly. Irene found in him an affable but confused individual endeavouring to come to grips with reality. When Anand wrote his confessions which ran into 2000 pages, Irene dutifully typed them out and even promised to marry him, if he found a publisher.

There are many significant events which effected a change in the perspectives of Anand's view of life. He viewed life not in abstract metaphysical terms, but in real terms, for he knew that the evolution of man towards future largely depends on the environment. Anand himself had undergone the severe tests of events, of class distinctions and his sympathy for the underdogs is thus not the product of a spasmodic outburst of emotions. Fortunately enough, Anand virtually participated in many of the important events which were strikingly revolutionary in intent and purport. For instance, the Coal Miners General Strike of 1925 in England, moved Anand very much; he plunged headlong into the maelstrom of struggle and deliberated with the British Trade Unionists with an intention to bring solace to the striking labourers. Apart from this, the alarming rise in unemployment, and consequent economic disequilibrium in the riot-torn England, forced Anand into joining the Marxian Circle. He had before him the glorious example of Soviet Russia marching towards a definitive future. Anand, almost with a righteous indignation, denounced the Fascist tendencies in Italy and Germany, and in the process, identified himself with the younger writers like Malraux, Auden, Spender and C. Day Lewis in order "to build a new healthy civilization on the reserve of enormous potential powers of good of human beings."[12] He even sang halleluahs in praise of October Revolution, under the sobering influence of the left-wing writers. He got his Doctoral Degree in 1929, and his search for an ideological fulcrum seemed to have been provided by Karl Marx's *Letters on India*, which acted as a catalyist in changing the whole perspective of Anand's outlook on life. As he observed :

> A whole new world opened to me. All the threads of my past reading which had got tied up into knots seemed suddenly to straighten out, and I

> began to see, not only the history of India, but the whole history of human society in some sort of inner connection...and, of course, the happiest thing was that Marxism was no dogma of church militant in spite of the culminators who declared to be another religion with Marx as its prophet — but a scientific and rational method for the study of society, a hypothesis which was leading in new discoveries.... Nothing less was involved than a re-orientation of one's outlook on history as well as a complete transformation of present day society from the new point of view.[13]

He started denouncing all right-wing politicians of Britain and found imperialism as abhorent and self-destructive. He formed, with Sajjad Zaheer, 'an outstanding member of the Central Committee of the Communist Party of India', a literary association called "The All-India Progressive Writers Association" in 1935, with the sole aim of infusing the Marxian content into contemporary Indian literatures. The Manifesto of the All-India Progressive Writers Association lays emphasis on presenting Social Realism in literature. As Margaret Berry points out :

> Accordingly, Progressive Writers were required to view subjects, characters, situations and attitudes as products of economic forces. Characters, in particular were to be treated as personifications of economic categories and embodiments of particular class relations. Situations ideally involved for masses in group struggle of economic emancipation. Attitudes were to reflect solid, unquestioning approval of all calculated to advance history towards an International Communist Society. Marxist social realism of the 'thirties left no room for doubt, questioning, or search relative to basic values and goals. These were *a priori* determined.[14]

Another significant event which boosted Anand's proletarian interest was his chance participation in the Spanish Civil War which well-nigh proved to be a purgatorial experience to him. He identified himself with the cause of the Republican Party and wrote a fascicule of pamphlets upholding the cause of the Communists, who were unflaggingly fighting against the formidable forces of fascism. In one of his articles, which served as a veritable document of his proletarianism, Anand observed :

> I am a novelist, a writer of books, of social documents, about a rather neglected country India. And, as I set from day-to-day writing a long novel about the peasants of my country while news of the Spanish War was coming in. I became conscious that the problem of agrarian masses of India was not very unlike that which faced the Spanish peasants, since both these people are emerging from feudalism, since both have for centuries been oppressed by a capricious landlordism, since both are face to face with the brutal tyranny of an upper class anxious to secure its privileges and possessions even if that involves the virtual extermination of the vast masses of the people.[15]

After his return to England, Anand still maintained his preference for the India League, and aligned himself with V.K. Krishna Menon, who had pronounced loyalty for Marxian Socialism. Thus, in his formative years Marxism became a veritable faith and a sacrosanct religion for Anand since it opened up new vistas for him. He was aware of the intrinsic merits of Marxian ideology and the role played by the intellectuals in the Russian Revolution, thus placing him in superior position in his country; besides, it provided security to him to those troubled times. When Anand started his literary career with the publication of his first novel *Untouchable* in 1935, he was a genuine Marxist, who "knew the truth", and he consciously used his art to propagate his new fangled ideas to the people. And in his major novels he hoped to align himself with the "disinherited, the weak and the dispossessed, as a human being and as an artist...to help transform society."[16] Though Anand had vehemently denounced capitalism in no less unequivocal terms, he had always pretended to be reticent and even deliberately ambivalent about his political leanings. So deeply was Anand influenced by Karl Marx's *Letters on India* that he edited them along with other material on colonialism and published them under the title *Letters on India.** As Saros Cowasjee observes :

> Anand sees it, Socialism alone can provide the right climate for man's total development. Thus, Marxism is the very cornerstone of Humanism,... Marxism does not reject the individual; man and his development is at the centre of Marxist thought. One must not lose sight of the close relationship between Marxism and Humanism in Anand's mind — in Anand's Mind — a relationship that is better evident in his works than in his numerous protestations. Furthermore, we must not allow ourselves to be cheated by Anand's generalizations or take undue interest in Anand's definitions, but we must look to their applications, not to theories or what he set out to do, but to what he actually achieved.

After settling down in India, Anand virtually changed his stance and started looking at everything in the new perspective. As Carlo Coppola rightly points out :

> The death of Stalin and the Khrushchev 'thaw' undoubtedly contributed to his change of attitutde. Ideology was now expressed in very broad, humanistic terms; revolution *per se* lost favour. Writer's individual liberties, the brotherhood of mankind, and peace and co-operation among nations were now the order of the day. Significantly, the All India Progressive Writers' Association, the Marxist-oriented literary organization founded in Lucknow in 1936, also reflected this change.[17]

Anand has written various articles comprising his ideas, literary theory and his views on life which made their way into *Apology for Heroism : A Brief Autobiography of Ideas* (1946), *New Bearings in Indian Literature* (1961), *Is There a Contemporary Indian Civilization?* (1963) *The Task Before the Writer* (1963), *Is Universal*

---

* In the Preface (p. 1), Anand recalls that he originally prepared the material for the press in 1933.

Criticism Possible? (1965), *A Note on Modern Fiction* (1965), *My Experiment with a White Lie* (1966), *The Role of the Writers and Artists in Developing Countries of Afro-Asian* (1968). It is worth pointing that before 1946, Anand wrote his major fiction and these articles were intended as critical offensives to absolve himself of the charge of 'commitment'. Anand has slightly changed his stand in the later phase of writing and started looking at everything differently, in the face of a global change in perspectives of the social life. He even accepted naively that he had come to socialism *via* Tolstoy, Ruskin, Morris and Gandhi as a protest against social anamolies which grippingly held the Indian masses all through the 'Thirties, and 'Forties.

Anand's aesthetic theory has its roots in the humanist tradition, within the conceptual framework of Marxism. He had founded the "All-India Progressive Writers Association" and later denounced 'Arts for Art Sake' school of writing as irrelevant since he felt that every writer is a committed writer one way or the other. As Chinua Achebe has observed, in another context : "Every writer is a 'committed' writer, one way or the other." "No book is", observed George Orwell "free from political bias. The opinion that art should have nothing to do with politics is itself a political attitude."[18]

With the publication of *Untouchable* in 1935, Anand shot into literary eminence and this was beginning of his career as a novelist. Then followed in a hectic succession, *Coolie* (1936), *Two Leaves and a Bud* (1936), *The Village* (1939) *Across the Black Waters* (1940), *The Sword and Sickle* (1942), *The Big Heart* (1945) beside two non-fictional works *Letters on India* (1942) and a long essay *In Search of Faith* (1943) which was later entitled *Apology for Heroism : A Brief Autobiography of Ideas*. The other novels include *Lament on the Death of a Master of Arts* (1938), *Private Life of an Indian Prince* (1953), *The Old Woman and the Cow* (1960), *The Road* (1960), and *Death of a Hero* (1963). He has also written a large number of short stories collections under the titles such as *The Lost Child and Other Stories* (1934). *The Barber's Trade Union and Other Stories* (1952) etc. and a book on *Persian Painting* (1930) and *Curries and Other Indian Dishes* (1932), *The Hindu View of Art* (1933).

Such is the prolific output as its variegatedness and one can guess the personality of the writer who turned them out, always wearing the benign mask to hide his ideology. Anand became a celebrity not only in India but also in the West. He was even asked to deliver lectures at the International PEN Conference, London; and his short stories were anthologized in *Writers in Freedom*. His articles found their way into the prestigious journals like *Tribune, The Listener, Fortnightly Review, The New Statesman, The Nation, Life and Letters, Labour Monthly* etc. His coterie of friends included E.M. Forster, Herbert Read, Bonamy Dobree, Aldous Huxley, T.S. Eliot, Lawrence Binyon, Stephen Spender, Middleton Murry, Louis MacNeice, V.S. Pritchett, George Orwell, Walter Allen, Dylan Thomas, C.D. Lewis, Virginia Woolf, H.G. Wells, Lowes Dickinson, Lawrence Durrell, Andre Malraux, Jack Lindsay etc. All these eminent men of letters have influenced him one way or the other. Anand still cherishes the warmth and affability he has shared with them.

Anand recalls rather painfully that there has not been any qualitative change in the social set up as envisioned by him. Asked about his communist affiliations, Anand denies that he is a hardcore Marxist though he shares in common with other moderates like E.M. Forster that 'no political creed except communism offers an intelligent man any hope'. Anand has found that his ideology to be lacking in the philip and is vexed to see Spender and Arther Koestler shying away from their ideological commitments and drifting towards a new philosophy which he prejoratively describes as 'revolutionary defeatism'. Anand's commitment to social radicalism makes him an activist engaged in championing the cause of Indian freedom under the guidance of socialist leaders like Mahatma Gandhi and Nehru. He has resented, in no uncertain terms, the imperialist hegemony of the Britishers. Though derided by the Progressive Writers Association in Bombay, he left for Soviet Russia to attend the Afro-Asian Writers Conference. In one of his letters to Saros Cowasjee, he recalls :

> I returned from the Gorky Centinary last week end. It was a wonderful experience because fifty world-writers were taken in a ship down the Volga river via Moscow canal, and the seminar was held in the boat under the relaxed conditions. Certainly,

> the honour paid to writers in the Communist world is something to be seen to be believed — in spite of the alleged bad treatment of recalcitrant! I tell them that if they could combine Communism with freedom of speech, they would usher an utopia.[19]

Today, Anand is busy completing his personal odyssey, the projected series of which four books have now come out in the book form, *Seven Summers* (1951), *Morning Face* (1976), *Confession of a Lover* (1976) and *The Bubble* (1984). He is also engaged in editing the prestigious *Marg*, a journal devoted to Fine Arts. His membership includes the P.E.N., Lalit Kala Academy, besides the membership of 'All-India Progressive Writers Association'. He is a regular contributor to some of the prestigious journals in India and abroad. Besides a fictionist, he is also a noted *belletrist.* He is an 'angry old man' still thundering at the doom of things, decrying the fascist tendencies, he still cares for the betterment of the underdogs of the India society. At present Anand is busying in writing a book on *Apartheid,* to help the African Fund to which our Prime Minister has promised to contribute.* He is a social reformer engaged in the crusading war against all forms of social oppression and religious authoritarianism. The famous Russian writer, Maxim Gorky once remarked :

> We are enemies, implacable, I am certain. An honest worker is always an enemy of society and even more an enemy of those who defend and justify agreed and envy, these base pillars of the modern social organisation.[20]

A similar recalcitrance and militancy and a passion for the establishment of a millennium of happiness gatecrash into the vitals of Anand's fiction. He does not have any elaborate aesthetic theory of the novel but has evolved his own mode of viewing at the novel, as an artistic communication of the real as well as the facsimile of the real. In his adoption of the technique of realism, with naturalistic

---

* In a personal letter to me Anand writes :

What time I have I am currently devoting to research on *Apartheid,* to help the African Fund to which our Prime Minister has promised to contribute.

(Mulk Raj Anand's letter dated 5th December, 1986.)

determinism as its corollary, he comes very near to the continental novelists like Balzac, Tolstoy and Maxim Gorky; but in the process he develops his own brand of "poetic realism". Anand merely carries on the technique of the indigenous brand of realism as evidenced in the novels of contemporary novelists like Prem Chand, Bankim Chandra Chatterjee and Yashpal, but steers clear of their gluey sentimentality and doctrinnaire opinions. He interprets the problems besetting man and society, and comes out with an adult view of life with his firm belief in the perfectability of man, in the "togetherness of life". As Dr. K.R. Rao rightly observes :

> Mulk Raj Anand, however, reveals a total commitment to socialist doctrine and gives credence to ideological analysis and humanistic evaluation. He merely presents a cross-section of Indian society through the national survey of the prevailing conditions in the twenties subordinates, rather than highlights, the historical experience.[21]

Anand firmly believes that a novelist should allow a free play of imagination in tracing out the antagonism between the emotional and physical life of human beings and desires very much that they should be left free to work out their own fate to undergo the processes of, what he calls, "Karma". As a staunch believer in the evolution of society towards a millennium happiness, Anand predicts an ambrosial future for mankind. And if this is a naive propaganda, all art is propaganda; the zeal with which it is worked out is all that is important for a novelist of Anand's stature. As Anand observes elsewhere :

> All art is propaganda. The art of Ajanta is propaganda for Buddhism. The art of Ellora is propaganda for Hinduism. The art of Western novel is propaganda for humanity against the bourgeois. Gorky as a humanist dared to speak of man, man's condition, not say how awful it is, but he also suggested what could be. And thus he did propaganda for man.[22]

REFERENCES

1. Mulk Raj Anand, *A Dialogue with M.A. Anand*, Studies in Mulk Raj Anand, Abhinav Pub., New Delhi (1986), p. 95.
2. Mulk Raj Anand, *Apology for Heroism,* Kutub-Popular, Bombay (1957), p. 9.
3. *Ibid.*, p. 78.
4. M.N. Roy, *New Humanism : A Manifesto*, Ajanta Publication, Delhi, (1981), p. 6.
5. Mulk Raj Anand, *Apology for Heroism,* Kutub-Popular, Bombay (1981), p. 91.
6. Iyengar, K.R.S., *Indian Writing in English*, Asia Publishing House, Bombay (1962), pp. 334-35.
7. M.K. Naik, *M.R. Anand,* Arnold-Heinemann, New Delhi (1973).
8. Mulk Raj Anand, *Apology for Heroism*, Kutub-Popular, Bombay (1957), p. 78.
9. *Ibid.*, p. 1.
10. *Ibid.*, p. 12.
11. Mulk Raj Anand, *Seven Summers,* Orient Paperbacks, New Delhi (1970), p. 140.
12. Mulk Raj Anand, *Apology for Heroism*, Kutub-Popular, New Bombay (1957), p. 21.
13. *Ibid.*, p. 22.
14. Margaret Berry, *M.R. Anand : The Man and the Novelist,* Oriental Press, Amsterdam (1974), p. 31.
15. Mulk Raj Anand, *The Invincible Will to Live*, Congress Socialist (29th May, 1937), p. 9.
16. Mulk Raj Anand, *Apology of Heroism*, Kutub-Popular, Bombay (1957), p. 91.
17. Carlo Coppola, *Politics and the Novel in India*. Orient Longman, Madras (1978), p. 3.
18. S.R. Bald, *Novelists and Political Conciousness,* Epigraph-Chanakya Publication, Delhi (1982).
19. Mulk Raj Anand, Letter to Cowasji, dt. 5th July, 1968.
20. Maxim Gorky, *Letter to Jean Richepin.* Articles and Pamphlets, Moscow (1950), p. 144.
21. Dr. K.R. Rao, *The Fiction of Raja Rao*, Parimal Prakashan, Aurangabad (1980), p. 4.
22. Mulk Raj Anand, *Speech,* Soviet Review, March 26 (1968), p. 62.

2

The Indian Inferno

Mulk Raj Anand's transition from revolutionary socialism to, what could be convincingly described as comprehensive 'historical humanism', is the result of his entrenched belief in the dictum that 'literature and life are parallel developments'.[1] For him, as for the other left-wing writers, social life around him provides the much-needed impetus, and his concern for the bottomdog or the socially depraved individuals remains the same even after the lapse of considerable time. Anand writes of the uncouchables, of coolies and of indentured labourers not with a view to bringing them into heroic stature; he is rather interested in charting out the progression of their journey from self-alienation to one of accommodation in a world where the springs of compassion are desiccated once for all. The heroes of Anand are in no sense the existential sufferers as it is made out to be, but the victims of the circumstance and they suffer not because of their *hybris* but because of their innate incapacity to defy the demands of the social order that has become so much insufficient as to be conceived as anachronistic. Anand is obviously much more concerned with as what Margaret Berry calls, 'the universal experience of man' than merely telescoping the topography or extending the symbolic typologies of and his environment. Anand is interested in charting out the individual's evolution from imminent destruction to the gradual processes of unfolding epiphany.

His first novel *Untouchable,* which has undergone several authorial prunings and revisions, is a powerful recordation of the life of an untouchable who becomes the victim of a society which denies him all possibilities of redemptive options only because he is 'low-born'. Although Anand had prepared the first draft in the span of 29 days, it is only at Gandhi's Sabarmati Ashram that the book took its final shape. Anand himself has observed : 'the book poured out like hot lava from the valcano of my courageous imagination.'[2] It is only after Anand has undergone the cathartic cleansing at Gandhi's Ashram that he has started writing his confessional which 'unleashed in Anand a torrent of specific memories of his childhood'.[3]

The hero of *Untouchable* is a sweeper boy, named Bakha, around whom the whole gamut of action moves. Anand skilfully grafts the Joycean technique of 'stream of consciousness' to his narrative and densely packs it with incidents and situations such that they acquire the lineaments of an epic as well as the symbolic centrality of a fable. He distances his art from overt propaganda and avoids all the ornate traceries of slipping into blatant proselytising. Though the book gets the tag, 'dirty', and as many as nineteen prospective publishers refused to publish it, it is accepted for publication only when E.M. Forster seemed to have given it a *carte blanche.* As he observes :

> *Untouchable* could only have been written by an Indian, and by an Indian, who observes from the outside. A European, sympathetic, could not have created the character of Bakha, because he would not have known enough about his troubles. And no untouchable could have written a book because he would have been involved in indignation and self pity.[4]

The novel opens in the *medias res,* as it were, with the spiritual crisis in the life of its protagonist Bakha, a sweeper boy of eighteen years, who is sound in mind and body. His routinized life begins with the horrendous abuses which he receives from his father and the diurnal cleansing of a row of latrines. Anand describes, almost with a painstaking particularity, the *malaise* of Bakha's unending drudgery. Three rows of latrines to clean single-handed that is Bakha's daily toil. His sister Sohini is also deft in her own way, though she decries the social stigmata. Anand describes her physical charms thus :

> She had a sylph-like form, not thin but full-bodied within the limits of graceful form, well-rounded on

> the hips, with an arched narrow waist from which descended the folds on her salwars and above which were her full, round, globular breasts, jerking slightly, for the lack of bodice, under her transparent muslin shirt. Bakha observed her as she walked along swaying. She was beautiful.[5]

When she goes to a community well to fetch water, she becomes embroiled in the unsuspected caste recriminations. One of the caste-Hindus, Kali Nath, draws water for her from the well and asks her to see him in the evening. Fascinated by her youthful charms, he makes improper advances at her in the courtyard of the temple, and she helplessly screams, the priest cries out 'polluted', 'polluted'. A crowd throngs upon the scene. Bakha tries to gauge the pitiful predicament of his sister, but remains a mute witness because of caste barriers, though he very much wanted to pull the priest out and beat him up.* He comes home and tells his father in a rather indignant but desperate tone : "They think we are mere dirt, because we clean their dirt."[6]

The spool of the story slowly unwinds itself through a series of denouements which occur in the life of the hero. Vexed and petrified by the subhuman treatment meted out to his sister, Bakha tries to compose in spite of himself. Another incident which sweeps him off the feet is the one in which he is slapped by a caste-Hindu for 'polluting' him. He fails to announce himself as usual and 'pollutes' a caste-Hindu unconsciously though and in return receives the torrent of abuses. This wounds him psychologically and makes him ponder over the humiliating segregation of man from man by the restrictive imperatives of a social order which has seemingly become anachronistic and irrelevant. Bakha did not mind scavenging for others; but what makes him invigil against the whole social system is the desire to see that it changes to accommodate ever one in its system. He has the potential to hit back, but his anger gets subsumed into an indifference and passivity as he becomes conscious of the fact that

* A few critics have interpreted Bakha's relationship with his sister in Freudian term. Bakha, as much as Kali Nath, has an incestuous desire to possess her, which is absurd.

a vast majority of outcastes too are subjected to the same kind of dehumanisation as he is. But two thousand years of continual suppression and intimidation of his race have not sapped out his humility, and he tries to suffer from these social indignities with an exemplary forebearance that is not untypical of a tragic hero. The only time when he is happy is that when his friend gives him a hockey-stick and when he good-humouredly apes the Tommies and their sortorial habits, since they treat him as a human being. This makes Bakha recognize the benevolence of the British Army Officers who seem to provide him temporary escape from the routine drudgery of life. Anand describes his hero, as he is caught in the glory of sunrise :

> He lifted his face to the sun, open-eyed for a moment, when with the pupils of his eyes half-closed, half-open. And he lifted his chin upright. It was pleasing to him. It seem to give him a thrill, a queer sensation which spread on the surface of his flesh where the tincture of warmth penetrated the numbed skin.[7]

This description reveals Anand's penchant for a brilliant evocation of the scene or event in order to surchage it with an inlaid potency that is in commensurate with the thematic gravitas. He has a remarkable sympathy for his hero who symbolises the predicament of a hapless victim pitted against the forces of orthodoxy and conservatism. In one of the incidents when Bakha receives both abuses and pancakes thrown at him by a housewife from the house-top, Anand seems to get the better hold to lay bare the real inhumanity to which the untouchables are subjected; they are treated as subhuman species 'between humans and dogs'. At the end of the novel, Anand suggests three solutions, which apparently seem too facile to be accepted as effective in reorienting the social perspectives : Bakha could become a Christian with the help of the Salvation Army Missionary, Hutchinson; he could hang his hopes on Gandhi's promise of eradication of the evils of untouchability; and the last, but not the least, the introduction of the water-closet, as promised by the poet, which makes the task of the sweepers easy. All these solutions are utopian in construct and seem to lack the efficacy to bring about a social change; but for Bakha they provide a bastion of hope and a redemption from the despicable drudgery afflicting the Indian society. Thus, the novel ends with a resounding note of optimism implied as it is in Bakha's adolescent dreams, when he sees an apostle in Gandhiji. Bakha's dream may come true or may not, but this life of unending toil goes on.

Anand also suggests, a fourth solution through a revolutionary leader, Bashir, who becomes the spokesman for all his ideas of social liberalism. As the poet says :

> We must destroy caste, we must destroy the inequality of birth and unalterable vocations. We must recognize an equality of rights, privileges and opportunities for everyone.... We must accept the machine which clears dung without anyone having to handle it — flush system. Then the sweepers can be free from the stigma of untouchability and assume the dignity of status that is their right as useful members of casteless and classless society.[8]

The poet harangues not only about the prospect of the emergence of a 'casteless' society but 'classless society', in which all distinctions get obliterated and the individual freedom is promised forth. Bashir, the Barrister-at-law, remarks : "In fact, greater efficiency, better salesmanship, more mass production, standardisation dictatorship of sweepers, Marxian materialism and all that"[9]; Anand's Marxian affirmations for the establishment of a gradualistic social liberalism thus gets crystallised. He desires the change to be 'organic' but not 'mechanical'.[10] Social in-equalities should be wiped out if at all the caste hierarchies are to be removed. In fact, Anand envisages a radical social transformation through revolution, not through the processes of continual evolution, which is slow and unsure. The poet, obviously endorses the novelist's ideas of the social utopia, as it were. He further observes :

> We can destroy our inequalities easily. The old, mechanical formulas of our lives must go; the old stereotyped forms must give place to a new dynamic.[11]

Thus, the very presence of Gandhiji, and his promise to

eradicate untouchability through the progressive measure of educating the people, reverberates in Bakha's mind. He dreams of a decent social life purged of all social evils and the novel ends with the resounding thud of optimism. The ending is as effective as the ending of Raja Rao's *Kanthapura*, though a few critics contend that the novel rather ends mid-way to serve Anand's propagandistic purpose. Prof. G.S. Amur, comparing the novel with Shivaram Karanth's *Choma's Drum,* observes :

> *Untouchable* is a novel in the mode of critical realism with the perceptible Marxist orientation while *Choma's Drum* steers clear of ideology and approaches the tragic mode. Anand's novel ends on a note of guarded optimism, while Karanth's precipitates into tragic conclusion...the inner form of both these novels is given by the tension between the interiority of the problematic hero and the contingent reality which is hostile to his aspiration.[12]

Nonetheless, Anand never tries to proselytise at the expense of artistic integrity but rather shows up various possibilities of the elimination of social barriers through the progressive assimilation of all into a conglomerate humanity. Anand is, nonetheless, interested in the spiritual evolution of his character, and Bakha's passage from innocence to experience is dramatized with a sensitivity that is in consonance with his creedal preoccupation. *Untouchable* is in no way a 'thesis' novel since its perspectives transcend both time and space as to en-core a wide social gesture of a revolutionary ardour which ordinates the feeling and experience. Bakha represents the 'dispossessed of the earth', the archetype of 'an expansive hero in a closed world', struggling to achieve perfection amidst chaotic world of perversion. The perception of Indian and nightmarish isolationism are akin to, what Kierkagard calls, 'the existential angst'. The novel deals not so much with the psycho-spiritual evolution as Bakha's corrosive rage and humiliation and his progressive graduation into a 'noble savage'. He is tested and formulated by a 'fore-closed society' in which the human choices become meaningless in seeming dichotomy of social forces. Bakha moves from self-disintegrating beast of burden to a higher state of awareness. He identifies himself not with his own caste of untouchables, but with a large chunk of humanity reeling under relentless forces of orthodoxy and conservatism. Thus, his meeting with Gandhiji is preludial to 'a new world of unbuying aspirations'. Anand dexterously charts out this process of self-individuation in Bakha, and his regaining of confidence and vigour in the face of abetting anomalies. Anand has neither contrived the situations nor character but has allowed them develop in course of narrative action in time, with his avowed aspirations for social redemption ordinating the whole perspective of the novel.

Judged from the vantage point, Bakha's alienation is both spiritual and social. The interlacing of both these strands lends to the narrative an epic sweep and immensity. Bakha's separation is not so much from the society which tries to dehumanise him as it is from himself. Like all the existential heroes whose suffering is self-engandered, Bakha too becomes the victim of fatality, within the confines of his social order. Anand's indictment is directed not against the individual, but against the whole society which refuses the individual's graduation and thwarts his attempts to lead an authentic life. Anand's novel is both a metaphor for life and an epic of suffering, for Bakha is both a representational figure and an individual trying to grapple with the forces of the aeons of orthodoxy and regimentation. Dr. K.N. Sinha observes :

> The novel has a tragic beauty of its own. The will to revolt and the sheer impossibility of successfully doing so under the circumstances constitute the basic tension in the novel. The hero is simultaneously a rebel and a victim. His anguish becomes our anguish, his sorrow our sorrow.[13]

Bakha, like many of the underdogs, tries to seek roots in a society where the springs of humanity and love seem to have desiccated once for all. In endeavouring to find a solution to his personal problems and overcome the 'crisis of consciousness', Bakha becomes not only a victim but also a victor, in the sense that he is able to put up with the thwarted purposings without sacrificing his innate potential to live in spite of the odds. His problem is one of frustrating sense of disinheritance and rootlessness. Anand, in fact, has created an 'Indian tragedy' analogous to the

'American tragedy' as does Dos Passos. Almost with a Dickensian realism and wry humour, Anand brings out the evils of an antiquated social order, which has obfuscated and blighted all avenues of individual betterment. As Marlene Fisher observes :

> Anand's novel, is at once and the same time a fine piece of creative work in terms of its own artistic integrity and an indiction of author's humanistic commitments and future novel.[14]

Commenting on the basic issues involved in the writing of the novel, Prof. C.D. Narsimhaiah has observed :

> In the novel (*Untouchable*) doctrine and dogmas are assimilated into a total sensibility which shapes his imagination and gives life an epoch and its hope and aspiration and its curse.[15]

Anand avoids all sorts of overt propaganda and sees that the novel develops along the character in action. His strict fidelity to the facts of life and a variety of the social mores make the novel at once a significant social document as well as a symbolic projection of the whole saga of human suffering. Bakha is put to a complex congeries of social realities, and the three incidents in which he finds himself unwittingly implicated, are keyed up to bring out the poignance in the life of his protagonist. Nonetheless, Anand finds no fault with the individual but faults the complicity of the society which assumes almost the Machiavellian proportions in denying humanity a sense of accommodation, solidarity and oneness. In the story of Bakha, Anand maintains a strict fidelity to the facts and traces out, through a series of unfolding epiphonies, the evolution of his character. As an omniscient narrator, Anand maintains a steady distance and uses every significant event in the service of art to cast more light on the character and the incident. Bakha is foredoomed to suffer, as all Anand's heroes, though in different circumstances. As in a Greek tragedy, *denouement* comes to the character through a powerful agency not outside of the social orbit. Anand is as much interested in tracing out the circumstances which lead to the hero's "shock of self-recognition" as with various forms of social cruelties to which his character is subjected. Even the three solutions which he suggests at the end of the novel —

Bakha's possible embracing of Christianity, Gandhiji's solution of eradication of untouchability and the introduction of the flush-system — may seem chimerical, if not impracticable. Anand could have suggested a radical transformation in the entire set-up of the Indian society. In fact, he was about to do it, but has to hold it in suspension because it is seemingly impossible to achieve these goals unless there is change from within. Even now, after fifty-two years of Independence, India is still reeling under the burden of caste-hierarchy, self-division and self-differentiation, and some of the recent incidents in Bihar, Uttar Pradesh and Andhra Pradesh have evidenced the outrage and havoc played by the caste-Hindus on the untouchables.* As Mulk Raj Anand observed elsewhere :

> In *Untouchable* the lives of the millions of the untouchables are as represented through one single person, only one incident *i.e.* the slap on the face evolved all the human relations, or many human relations, of the sixty-five millions of people whom the hero represents against the millions of caste-Hindus. The essence of the situation of Bakha lies in this insult as in Dostoevsky's *Insulted and Injured*, as in Tolstoy's *Hadji Murad.*[16]

Anand's novel seems to follow a set pattern of a tragic drama, incorporating into the structure, beginning with agon, peripeteia and an aganorsis, with the principal figure always undergoing all these processes of triple transmutation. The protagonist is put to severe ordeals which often lie outside his social parameters. Though he has the potency to revolt and to be wilfully belligerent, he is snubbed and subdued by the rigidities of social custom. It is obvious that Anand the propagandist, comes to the fore and Anand

* In the year 1985, the incident which took place in a small town called Keramchedu in Andhra Pradesh, shows up the age-old feud and the internal bickerings between the Harijans and Caste-Hindus which sparked off violent and outrageous exhibition of might on both sides. The Harijans were beaten-up, maimed and killed because, they defying the village head-man's directive, attempted to draw water from the well. The incident shook the whole State and it was reported that the Harijans feared to go back to their native places and wanted to be rehabilated elsewhere, far from the township they lived in, for fear of repraisals.

the artist, is baffled by the very aplomb he has generated into his narrative. Dr. K.R. Rao observes :

> Anand is merciless in his exposures of the evil elements in the social structure and his sociological indictment has a disturbing logicality which admits no timid caveats of gradualistic liberalism. Bakha's quest for identity in a world which refused to recognize him, has been traced by the novelist with a touch of sympathy as well as a lacerating irony. Anand's condemnation of untouchability derives its strength from his passionate involvement in, and identification with, the problems of the socially-boycotted individuals. He shows the utter futility of attaching a tag and wants us to recognize the fact that the untouchable is primarily a human being, who is 'the flesh of our flesh and the blood of our blood'.[17]

Anand's novel retains the classical purity of form and conforms strictly to twentyfour hour duration, the climatic scene being one in which Bakha is slapped by a caste-Hindu providing a kind of lynchpin to the whole narrative for unfolding epiphany. As in James Joyce's *A Portrait of the Artist As a Young Man*, Anand uses the omniscient narration and examines, almost with an ingratiating temper and inwardness, the plight of untouchables in India. And he is in fact writing not so much about the untouchables as about the "metaphoric untouchables" of all cultures. The novel is thus concerned both with the individual and collective emancipation as well from all kinds of vestigial social anomalies, repressions and perversities. As Anand himself has stated elsewhere :

> (The hero is) a rare human being whom I had known from my childhood and adored as a hero because he was physically like a god, played all the games superbly, and could recite whole cantos from the epic poem Heer Ranjah of Waris Shah....
> I was not however, remembering him in boy's own paper mood of hero worship. Even on the level of commonsense reality, I was aware and his tragedy. That this otherwise near perfect human

> being was a sweeper who was always being humiliated by most of our elders on account of his low caste, was not allowed to go to school, even if his father had sent him (which he would not have) flawed his excellence, for no fault of his. And though patronized because he was a good worker and obedient, he was suspected of leading all the young people astray and therefore was vigilantly watched and kept at the bay. The contradiction between the inborn qualities of his youth and the down, and out status to which he was condemned, may have been the cause of my brooding about him.... I glimpsed the truth that the tragedy of my hero lay in the fact that he was never allowed to attain anything near the potential of his qualities of manhood.[18]

He feels that no amount of social legislation will solve the problems besetting the underdogs and so his protagonist becomes a passive witness to all the acts of caste insurgencies played out upon him by the caste-Hindus. Bakha's passivity is born of disenchantment; but still there is an achieved poise in him, a *sang froid* that comes only to an individual who is tested by all the forces of the accumulated fury and tyranny of the age-old social customs which divide man from man. As Prof. K.R.S. Iyengar sums up the novel :

> *Untouchable* strikes us as the picture of the place of a society, and the certain persons not easily to be forgotten; a picture that is also an indictment of the evils of a decadant and perverted orthodoxy. As a novelist addressing himself to the task of exposing certain evils, Anand (it must be conceded) has been as effective as Dickens himself.[19]

If Anand's *Untouchable* gives us the microcosmic vision of life in India, *Coolie* is more like a macrocosm. Both in its conception and rendition, *Coolie* sensitively portrays the Indian life, with all its time-tested social customs and traditional taboos. Though the novel is meant to give a cross-section of the people, the lowly and the rich, the bewildered and bedevilled, it in fact represents more than the Indian social life. With almost a Dickensian nerve and gusto, Anand projects, once again, the plight of the *les miserables* pitted against the backdrop of social malaise. He looks forward to the development novel aided by the fictional contingencies of realism and naturalistic determinism. Munoo is the central character in *Coolie*. He is one among the millions of coolies, tested and formulated by a myriad forces of class distinctions, exploitation and dehumanisation. If, in *Untouchable*, the caste plays a significant role in undermining the evolution of the hero into self-individuation, in *Coolie* it is the class distinction that disinvigorates the individual's attempts at self-survival. Both the systems are pooh-poohed by Anand who seems to endorse the view that as long as these caste and class rigidities prevail in the Indian society, the redemptive options open for the individual betterment become thwarted. He in fact looks forward to a society based on equity and broad-based humanism, a system which recognises the intrinstic worthiness of an individual which allows him retain his 'species character'. That is precisely the reason why he envisions a conglomerate society where all class distinctions are merged into one comprehensive humanistic ideal which promises forth openness and freedom.

The story of Munoo is quintessentially the story of every exploited individual in India and the patterns of his life are intended to show the pitilessness that lies imbeded in the lives of millions of people who are condemned to lead a life of an unending saga of social depradation. The plight of coolies or the indentured labourers is dramatised with such a fiery pointedness and ferocity that the very thought of it provokes a revulsion against the society which refuses to acknowledge them or allow them to lead a life of their own, however lackluster it may be. Anand charts out Munoo's sojourns from a comparatively small idyllic village to a cosmopolitan city like Bombay, and then unto Simla where he dies of consumption at the age of fifteen, 'unsung and unwept'. Munoo is presented as an orphan who lives under the tutelage of his fussy uncle, and equally loveless aunt. His uncle takes him to Babu Nathoo Ram's house at Sham Nagar in order to free him from the octopus-grip of his nagging aunt. But paradoxically enough, Munoo has to confront a far more formidable Bibiji who abuses him every time, without any reason. He finds himself translated into a sort of a veritable inferno and more cruelties and threats are in store for him. He finds a compassionate friend in Chota Babu, but fails to put up with the virago, Nathoo Ram's wife. He providentially escapes from Nathoo Ram's house only to find himself in the company of Prabha, who takes him to Daulatpur. Munoo's life takes yet another unsuspected turn. With the unquenchable optimism and excitement, he starts working in the pickle factory owned by Prabha and finds solace in the company of the co-workers, and gains sympathy from Prabha and his wife, more than in ample measure. The Cat Killers Lane, which is a veritable den, still seethes with contradicting pulsations of life, the little joys, interspersed with drudgery and psychological ruptures. Unfortunately for Munoo, his proprietor lands himself in bankruptcy, which results in the untimely but sudden closure of the pickle factory.

Munoo is on the streets once again; he becomes a coolie in the grain market, a porter in a railway station and a factotum doing all sorts of sundry jobs. By sheer coincidence, he comes in contact with an elephant-trainer in the Circus who takes him to Bombay, which later proves to be an 'unreal city' for him. He finds himself in a factory working as a coolie and is forced to live among the slum dwellers in sub-human conditions. He is exposed to the pitiless cruelties of poverty and misery, and all sorts of mental and physical afflictions which render him a hapless victim of exploitation. He says that the society has only two types of people—the poor and the rich, the abyss that can never be bridged. Though he finds winsome comaradrie and *bonhomie* in the large-souled Hari, who treats him as a fellow human being, the factory owners have no sympathy for him. The trouble surfaces for him even here, and the factory is closed down because of the indefinite strike collectively organised by the workers; Munoo is later caught in the melee of mingling cross-currents of skirmishes slogan-mongerings which later assume thc proportion of a global war of class-conflict. He tries to escape from this inviolable involvement in thc Hindu-Muslim disturbances and runs up to Malabar Hills and gets eventually knocked down by a car. The owner of the car, Mrs. Mainwaring, takes Munoo to Simla where he becomes her page; but later he dies of consumption, having touched the nadir of despair.

Thus, the prominent theme of Anand's novel in *Coolie*, is the theme of 'lost innocence' as it is related to the personal life of the protagonist who finds no silver line in the horizon of life. Munoo is akin to Bakha in more than one respect; he is innocent and warm-hearted and has a remarkable zest for life. Munoo is aware of the fact that the whole society is based on 'the cash-nexus', and he is forced to play out his role as a coolie, a rickshaw-puller and a page to Mrs. Mainwaring, who is a woman of many pretences. The novel ends with Munoo's death, the metamorphical orphan, who never gains his rightful accommodation in his society. Anand observes :

> In the early hours of one unreal, white night he passed away — the tide of his life having reached back to the deep.[20]

Anand considers his novel as 'metaphor for life snuffed out', as well as an indictment on colonialism written in the mould of Kipling's *Kim.* Apparently, the novel's focused intensity is located in its virulant assaults on capitalism and the attendant horrors and evils it has brought about. The four phases in the life of his hero, his experiences in the house of Nathoo Ram, his escaps to Bombay, where he becomes initiated into the profession of labourer in a pickle-factory and then on as a worker in Sir John Cotton Mills, and finally, his stay at Simla with Mrs. Mainwaring where he succumbs to tuberculosis, all form the main patterns of the narrative. They are intended to forge not merely the vicissitude in the life of an individual but collective life as well. Munoo is a naive, hill-boy who tries to look forward to decency in life, but never does he attempt to grapple with the larger reality of the Indian social life. In his innocent self-certitude, he tries to know the causes of his disorientation, but strangely becomes the very archetype of suffering humanity. As Riemenschneider points out :

> Munoo is not the common type of hero or protagonist we expect to find in ... a novel in his opposition to society he is passive while society is active. Munoo does not build his own life which, on the contrary, is built for him.[21]

Thus, the story of Munoo is the story of an unending pain relieved only by some imperfect glimpses of happiness. His spirit never sags nor his indomitable will becomes extinguished. Munoo continues his relentless struggle even amidst the welter of pain and laceration with the unflagging spiritedness and honesty to redeem himself from 'death-in-life' predicament.

Munoo is disinherited or becomes dispossessed even when he becomes conscious of it. Anand is as much interested in tracing out the initiation of his here into experiential awareness as in charting out the processes of his continual exploitation. Munoo's search for a foothold in a society that has ill-treated him and his failure to come out of the solipsistic circle which restricts his growth, constitutes the main patterns in the novel. But paradoxically though, before he blooms into fullness of life, he becomes the victim of the cruel fate which thwarts all his purposings and leaves him a scape-goat. His life gets eroded by this pitiless social custom, and he becomes exploited all through his life. Thus, Anand's protagonist becomes the victim of other people's greed, arrogance, cruelty, a victim, as it were, of 'civilization'.

Many critics regard *Coolie* as basically a "proletarian novel", with its centrality now shifted onto the predicament of working-class. As in the first novel, *Untouchable,* in his second novel too, Anand makes a frontal attack on the capitalist system directly through the character of Sauda, the leader of Red Flag Union of workers. As he observes :

> "There are only two kinds of people in the world; the rich and the poor", Sauda continued, "and between the two there is no connection. The rich and the powerful, the magnificent and the glorious, whose opulence is built on robbery and theft and open warfare, are honoured and admired by the whole world, and by themselves. You, the poor and humble, you the meek and the gentle, wretched that you are dwindled out of your rights, and broken in body and soul. You are respected by no one and you do not respect yourselves.[22]

He further brings out the contrast between the lives of capitalists and the poor labourers of cotton mills in such a fashion as to evoke revulsion, if not total apathy against all the processes of exploitation. He says :

> They are robbers, the thieves, the brigands, the brigands who live in palatial bungalows on the Malabar Hills, on the money you earn for them with your work.... They eat five meals a day and issue forth to take air in the large Roll-Royes.[23]

As all revolutionary idealists, are aware of the fact that labourers are exploited even before they become conscious of the nature of exploitation. He tries to arouse them from age-old drudgery and bored apathy into active participation such that they can atleast become freed from the bondage of slavery.[24] As a revolutionary messiah, he attempts to organise masses into a collective revolt which is also the seminal thrust of Anand's thesis in the novel.

> Stand up then, stand up for your rights, you roofless wretches, stand up for Justice; Stand up, you frightened fools. Stand up and fight. Stand up and be the men that you were meant to be and don't crawl back to the factories like the worms that you are ! Stand up for life, or they will crush you and destroy you altogether. Stand up and follow me! From tomorrow you go on strike and we will pay you to fight your battle with the employers. Now stand up and recite with me the charter of your demands.[25]

Thus Anand's diatribe against capitalism comes out unobtrusively. His flair for revolutionary idealism and his desire to restore to the bottomdogs both human dignity and decorum, and the vestigial glory, assumes almost the purport of pulpit oratory. Anand shows, through the interaction of character and action as to how the individuals are crushed before they become aware of the soulless exploitative system. Munoo, like Bakha, suffers all social indignities but retains in him a certain unbuyable integrity which makes him the 'paragon of animals'. While for Bakha, realisation comes through a series of epiphanies, for Munoo knowledge comes through unrelieved sufferings. He realizes the fact that the root cause of suffering is class-distinction, an evil which seems to have assumed a global proportion in the Indian social system. He also comes to know that the hiatus between the rich and poor is wide enough as to become deeply entrenched in the social hierarchy. Munoo is the very archetype of the millions of unfortunate coolies who could be termed as India's 'lost generation', condemned to lead the life full of unresolved contradictions and unrelieved pains.

Anand believes that poverty by itself is a cruelty perpetuated by the *nouveau riche*. Munoo becomes the victim of exploitation and people like Daya Ram, Nathoo Ram, Ganpat, Chimta Saheb and Mrs. Mainwaring exploit him, though occasionally they try moderation, if not total antipathy towards the 'have-nots'. The capitalist system, buttressed by the 'cash nexus' and exploitation, unleashes several emotional crises and leaves the labourers entrapped in a peculiar predicament. In one of the finest passages, Anand describes Munoo's life in the dark chambers of pickle factory at Daulatpur :

> It was a dark and evil life. He (Munoo) rose early at dawn before he had his full sleep out, having gone to bed long before midnight. He descended to work, in the factory, tired, heavily heavy-lidded, hot and limp, and if all the strength had gone out of his body and left him a spineless ghost of his former self.[26]

With almost the Dickensian penchant for rugged details, he presents the sordid facts in the life of the labourers, inhabiting the slums as its scums. Anand observes :

> The bodies of numberless coolies lay strewn in tattered garbs. Some were curled up in knots others lay face downwards on folded arms, others were flats on their chests, pillowing their heads on their bundles or boxes, other crouched into the corners talking, other still huddled together at the doorsteps of closed shops, or lay on boards, in a sleep which looked like death, but that it was broken by deep sighs.[27]

Munoo comes to know from the elephant driver of the circus

the sordid facts of life; 'The bigger a city is, the more cruel it is to sons of Adam. You have to pay even for the breath that you breath'.[28] He finds Bombay to be :

> ...a land of cruel contrasts, where the bybric pomp of the rich mingled with the smell of sizzling grease in black frying-pans. Bombay, land of luxury and lazzaroni, were all the pretences of decency ended in dirt and drudgery, where the lies of benevolent patrons were shown up in the sores and deformities of poor.[29]

The plight of coolies in the cotton mill is no less infernal and Anand describes the apathy and cussedness of the capitalists in a tone that borders on pitiless cynicism :

> The coolies of the Sir George White Factory crept like ghosts through the waste lands of the mills...that little spark of life with which made them move about willingly had died, and left them a queer race of men, dried up, shrivelled, hollow-chested, hollow-cheeked, hollow-eyed. Their wretchedness had passed beyond the confines of suffering and left them careless, resigned.[30]

He catalogues the interminable woes of the working class in the Sir George White Factory at Bombay and shows how the big bosses from Britain control the whole machinery. The coolies are exploited beyond redressal; they are often under-paid and even forced to live the life of subhumans condemned perpetually to live in unhygienic slums, where they are huddled up like animals. In the description of the slums of Bombay, there is almost a photographic fidelity and miniscular precision and accuracy of detail.

> ...there were only corpses lying around some on their sides, others on their backs; still others facing downwards, all contracting their limbs to occupy the smallest place and bound up like knots of anguish where every breath seems to ask the elements for the gifts of sleep.[31]

Anand seems to imply that the human beings are not only huddled up, but they have been stolen into the animal world. The colour of their bodies is akin to the colour of the earth. Nonetheless, Anand's proletarian interest which surfaces, time and again mars the novel's selfhood though he maintains his poetic realism. In the first novel, *Untouchable*, Anand atleast strikes a balance between his art and propaganda; but in the present novel, he seems to lose his control over the material. This explains for the sprawling content of the novel and the blowing of the perspectives. But where Anand succeeds eminently in the presentation of the cross-section of the Indian social life and the travails of the lowly, which lend to the novel a genuine inwardness which is rare in Indian fiction in English. As Prof. C.D. Narsimhaiah observes :

> Contrasts, reinforcements, parallel situations seem to be an important part of Anand's technique in concretizing in words of patterns of life which he knows best.[32]

Many critics concede to the fact that all major novels of Anand are written with specific artistic purpose, but *Coolie* is the only novel which is downright propaganda. Though the novel presents the plight of a proletarian hero abetting the environmental fate, Anand's over enthusiasm to drive his message home heavily hangs on the artistic pattern, thus tending to make the novel an assemblage of personalities, events and inanities. As S.C. Harrex observes :

> *Coolie* demonstrates an early tendency in Anand to present life in terms of proletarian experience and a commentary on the experience, and these two aspects are artificially separated at certain points of authorial intrusion or didactic characterisation because of the intellectual limitation of the central character.[33]

In the third novel *Two Leaves and a Bud*, with its scene now shifted to the Assam tea plantations owned by the Britishers, Anand tries to explore the human predicament in all its variegatedness and amplitude. But the earlier vehemence of rage seems to have lost its pungency in the present novel since his over-enthusiasm seems to lean heavily on the dramatisation of the plight of the indentured labourers. In the result, he produces a 'thesis novel', which oversteps the parameters of aesthetic and artistic credibility. The scathing comment on the society, which now assumes the global form of a racial conflict, is meant to underscore the attendant horrors of discrimination it generates. But curiously enough, Anand pays very little attention to develop his characters or objectify his vision and social concerns. His characters, especially the British characters, appear as mere caricatures rather than genuine human beings. The total impression that one gets of the novel is an artistic failure which is often adduced to Anand's overt propaganda at the expense of fictional authenticity and veracity.

In *Two Leaves and a Bud*, we are back again in the menacing Macherson Estate in distant Assam. The central character in the novel is a middle-aged Gangu, who is the very archetype of beleaguered humanity. Gangu moves alongwith his family, from Hoshiarpur in Punjab to the far off Assam to eke out his livelihood. He is recruited by Sardar Buta to work in the tea plantations under some false allurements and Gangu dreams of a promised glory for him as for his children :

> I suppose it was in our kismet. But at the time it was like a prison and here it is slightly worse.... 'First water, afterwards mire'. This prison has no bars, but is nevertheless and unbreakable jail. The Chowkidars go around at night with a lamp and open every door to see if we are all at home. There used to be a roll call every night.[34]

The narrative centres round the basic conflict between the exploiter and the exploited, the one collectively represented by the Indian indentured labourers, and the other by the British colonisers. There are massed polarities, too, implied in the novel, the exploiter and the exploited, the black and the white, the good and the bad. Most of the Indian characters are represented as naive and innocent victims of the British colonialism, with the exception of a few British characters like Croft-Cooke and Reggie Hunt, the Assistant Manager, who are represented as the stooges of British imperialism; crooked and nefarious Croft Cooke and Reggie Hunt are the very embodiments of evil, presaging the very phantasmagoria unleashed by the forces of imperialism. Soon after his arrival at tea-plantations Gangu realizes that he has been trapped in a pandemonium without escape routes and he seems to loose his grip on his own innate potentiality. Suddenly malaria breaks out in the colony and his wife Sajani becomes its first casualty. He goes to the plantation owner Croft-Cooke seeking for help, but comes back home insulted and kicked out. Then, Gangu goes to Sardar Buta Ram, who refuses to advance him loan. He later meets Dr. John de la Havre who has pronounced sympathy for the coolies and gets succour. Gangu, having lost his wife, drifts from bad to worse and finds no peace at heart.. He starts living at the mercy of his masters, having lost the sustaining faith in his future. Discontentment and disenchantment in life make him a destitute trying to embattle with the malevolent forces of continual repression and exploitation. Suddenly a quarrel breaks out between the two loose women, which later turns into a huge demonstration of forces in which the coolies are divided into two camps. Anand describes the scene with utmost fidelity.

> The crowd was uncontrolable, gesticulating wildly. Men joined their hands in humility or raised their arms menacing, swearing, cursing and begging. 'I will shoot you all' Reggie roared, 'I will shoot you all if you dare to lift a hand or foot....'

Reggie turned imputuously, and hurled himself towards them.

> 'Strike them,' he yelled to the warders, 'Strike them'. And with his lips tight, and his head strung into wooden hardness, he rode his horse into the thick of the crowd, trampling on the men, women and children and pushed and grovelled and run in utter confusion. The frightened mob screamed and rushed and grovelled and run in utter confusion. The frightened mob screamed and rushed in frantic dismay, but he rode straight at them....
>
> The warders rushed upon the stricken coolies, and dealt blind, and haphazard blows in all directions...till their blows had tired their hands.[35]

Hell is let loose, confusion unleashing disorder. Dr. Havre is informed of the incident in which a coolie is killed. Dr. Havre sympathises with them and asks them to represent their grievances to the Manager. Reggie Hunt roars at them :

> Hands up! Hands up! pointing his revolver at the

> ring leaders. Warders, march these men back to their houses. Take them off before I shoot them all! The warders came forward and began to drive the men with the barrel ends of their rifles...they dug the ends of their rifles into them still more menacingly.
>
> Some of the crowd had already turned and ran. The rest fell back stumbling, shrieking, hysterical craven and defeated.[36]

The plantation owner, fearing that the mutiny of coolies is imminent, seeks the military help and the demonstrators are brow-beaten and brought to their senses. Reggie Hunt, who feels humiliated, nurtures ill-will against the whole community of the coolies. One day Reggie Hunt sees Leila, the daughter of Gangu, plucking the leaves, and in order to avenge Gangu, he reaches Gangu's house and tries to molest her. Emotions well-up and the scuffle follows in which Gangu is shot dead, thus bringing the unending saga of pain to a logical conclusion. What ensures later is a mock trial consisting of the seven European and two Indian members of the jury who find Reggie Hunt 'not guilty'.

Thus, the novel ends on a note of unrelieved pain and disenchantment and sombre foreboding. Anand pours out his vitroil on the colonisers who treat the natives as sub-humans. Though it is done at the cost of artistic integrity, he succeeds in a little measure to keep up his realism and humanistic sympathies in tact. It is one of the most gory novels ever written by Anand, the macabre and the starkly real, jostling into the narrative continuum or their fictional enactments; he seems to be pre-occupied with the proletarian ideology more than the need to be artistically viable. John Brophy points out : "The novel is purely Left-wing propaganda poured white hot in the mould of fiction."[37] It is a truism to say that the novel is mainly intended to be an indictment on capitalism as it belongs to the ethos prevailing in the 1930's. Anand is thoroughly inspired by the Marxian phase which was a principal utopian construct in those years even as the American novelists like Upton Sinclair, Dos Passos and Steinbeck. So passionate was his commitment to radicalism that Anand was impelled to graft and re-orientate his ideas into Marxian mould. The story of Gangu is thus patterned to signify human endeavours for betterment, for decorum in life. Anand himself observes elsewhere, 'it was a real story which he was writing in thinly veiled fiction'. He further goes on to say : 'the catharsis of a book lies ultimately in the pity, compassion and understanding of an artist, and in the partiality'. In fact, the whole narrative is keyed up to show the lone man fighting against the forces of environmental fate, against the forces of capitalism. It is essentially a proletarian novel, like its predecessor *Coolie*, where class consciousness overweighs the individual endeavours at self-survival. As in *Coolie*, the present novel gives us, almost in telling details, the panoramic picture of the tea-plantations in Assam. Anand describes the sunrise on the Assam tea-plantation thus :

> The morning mist had risen over the valley and evaporated with the dazzling burst of sunlight. The air was still under the clear even sky. The welter of leafage was tense beneath the world's hollow cup. There was a concentrated lull in the slow heart of the day, as if India missed a heart beat of the day, in the march of time.[37]

The plantation estate is owned by the Britishers; their sole aim is to spread their imperialistic hegemony everywhere. The honest labourers are often put to grilling toil and subjected to live in unhygienic conditions. They have neither recognition as humans nor free will to exercise. In one of the passages in *Apology for Heroism*, Anand makes his *obiter dicta* obvious.

> It never seems to have entered the heads of our masters to give the coolies the slightest chance of bettering themselves. They worked from dawn to dusk, old and young, male and female for their masters, they were treated like dogs.[38]

The novel is, by the large, a success in fictional terms in its documentation and in its vivisection of the degree and measure of exploitation. Anand's spokesman in the novel is Dr. John de la Havre, who had pronounced sympathies for the exploited labourers and he even submerges his identity for the sake of the proletariats. Most of his ideologies and comments reveal Anand's own ideological preferences and proletarian bias. Dr. Havre has given up the Imperial Medical Service and has come to the Assam tea-plantations with a mission to serve the poor and the needy. As Anand points out :

> He (Dr. Havre) had really come to regard human beings and to believe that they had a right not only to rule themselves, but to rule themselves justly by destroying the inequalities of caste, class and creed.[39]

In the Ninteenth Chapter of the novel, there is a lengthy discussion between Barbara and Dr. Havre on the need for global revolution. As Dr. Havre observes :

> Few are burdened with the kind of thoughtful imagination, patience and insight which is required to create a coherent world society...hundreds of men in the I.M.S. have passed by India except Roos (Russia), perhaps. But why didn't need to read Marx to realize here. The black coolies clear the forest, plants and the fields, toil and garner the harvest, while all the money-grubbing, slave-driving soulless managers and directors draw their salaries and dividends and build up monopolies. Therein lies the necessity of revolution in this country.[40]

As in the two preceding novels, *Untouchable* and *Coolie*, in the present novel too, Anand feels the necessity of a total revolution to wipe out the class-distinctions. The pathetic plight of the conditions of the labourers in India is vividly portrayed in *Two Leaves and a Bud* :

> The position of the plantation coolies in India is in many respects, similar to that of cotton plantation slaves of Southern States of North America...the present economic condition of Indian Coolies worse than was that of the negro slaves in America.
>
> The present system of plantation labour... is a curse and a crime. It is monstrous crime against humanity.[41]

Most of the labourers are Indians and the plantation owners are invariably the whitemen, who ill-treat the subject citizens with little clemency, because of racial hatred. The way in which Gangu is denied his rightful position to lead a decent life, out of lacerating anxieties shows the pity of it all. Anand's thesis is that redemption for the millions of Indian labourers comes through the betterment of living conditions by means of appropriate economic and social legislation. The age-old division of the society into two classes — the pleasure-seeking affluent class and the toiling masses is evidently pathetic and the masses deserves a better deal. The yawning gulf between the rich and the poor cannot be bridged except by the possible removal of the British imperialism from India which guarantee for them both political emancipation and economic liberalism. Anand seems to inveigh against the whole system of exploitation and sympathise with the lot of the 'have-nots' who suffer abject poverty, humiliation, and depradation. Gangu thus becomes not only the victim-hero but the very symbol of human suffering. Like Munoo, he moves from pillar to post in search of 'livable place' but simply remains numb with passivity and indifference; he accepts miseries heaped upon him, like most of the victim heroes of Anand's early novels. Anand puts this process of dehumanisation thus : 'there is nothing more horrible in this universe than the cruelty of man to man'. Thus, *Two Leaves and a Bud* is a bleak novel, with no possible hope of redemptive options left for the individuals. As S.C. Harrex observes :

> *Two Leaves and a Bud* is a dark novel, it is not without hope. There is hope, Anand implies, while there are people like de la Havre to put their moral strength against the social forces of darkness.... Taken together *Untouchable, Coolie, Two Leaves and a Bud*, indicate that in the Thirties Anand was developing a conception of Indian novel as an essentially proletarian work.[42]

The plot of *Two Leaves and a Bud* is so conceived as to intercut various themes, especially those of the historical process of imperialist hagemony and the pitiless exploitation of the masses, bordering on inhumanity. The conflict between the two racial groups assumes a further particularity and autochthonous pulsation since the whole drama is meant to re-enact the plight of the underprivileged, yoking under the burden of unmitigated lacerations. The story of Gangu, who is meted out to inhuman treatment, and his ultimate death, are meant only to reveal the potency, horror and ugliness of the racial conflict under the aegies of the British Raj.

Anand succeeds in portraying the British characters, particularly Reggie Hunt, who is represented as the very embodiment of evil. He eminently succeeds in painting Reggie's aggressive, neurotic behaviour, and physiological egoism and all the animal drives like lust and power which make him a stilted stereotype. He reminds us of yet another character typecast by Manohar Malgaonkar in the name of Henry Winston in *Combat of Shadows*. The only character who seems to be authentically credible is Dr. la Havre, who typifies Anand's idealistic euphoria. But even here, Anand seems to lose his grip over the material and his characters degenerates into mere caricatures. Other character such as Croft-Cooke, Hitchcock and Major Barbara are presented as typical British characters, 'with no flesh and blood complexity'. They are meant to be carboard figures with no functional relevance or symbolic thrust. Anand seems to have 'sought to grapple directly with the theme of conflict as a group experience',[43] and in the process, blunts all the edges of the novel, with proletarian propaganda. In portraying Gangu's character, yet another of his archetypal victim-hero Anand largely succeeds in keeping up both veracity and authenticity of his character without mincing details. Gangu's story is essentially the story of an individual's progression from dreary ugliness of life into yet another fussilade of sordid pattern of life. Gangu's experience as an indentured labourer and his continual exposure to the cynical cruelties of life make him a subhuman beast. His progressive alienation from the society in which he lives and his stoic acceptance of fatality, typify the predicament of an Indian labourer who is, as Malcolm Darling observes 'is born in debt, live in debt and dies in debt'. Anand has not resented the charge that he has shown partiality in portraying the Indian characters as all white and the British characters as all black. Perhaps Anand wanted to do something like E.M. Forster in *A Passage to India*, but he has simply failed to objectify his perceptives. Thus, his novel dwindles into a proletarian diatribe, without a firm footing in the collective experience, and one doesn't know where exactly Anand's art begins and his propaganda starts asserting itself. It is difficult to estimate the strength of the novel though Saros Cowasjee says that 'its latent weaknesses are its strength'.

NOTES

1. Mulk Raj Anand, *Author to Critic,* The Letters of Mulk Raj Anand to Saros Cowasjee, Writers Workshop, Calcutta (1973), pp. 14-15.
2. Mulk Raj Anand, *My Experiments with a White Lie,* Indian Literature, Vol. X, No 3 (1967), p. 20.
3. Marelene Fisher, *The Wisdom of the Heart : A Study of the Works of Mulk Raj Anand*, Sterling Publications, New Delhi (1985), p. 25.
4. Mulk Raj Anand, *Untouchable* — Preface, Arnold-Heinemann, New Delhi (1982), p. 9.
5. *Ibid*., p. 26.
6. *Ibid*., p. 89.
7. *Ibid*., p. 98.
8. *Ibid*., p. 132.
9. *Ibid*., p. 173.
10. *Ibid*., p. 173.
11. *Ibid*., p. 173.
12. G.S. Amur, *Essays on Critical Literature and Linguistics* : Ed. G.S. Amur, Sterling Pub., New Delhi (1984), p. 118.
13. M.N. Sinha, *Mulk Raj Anand*, Twayne Pub., Inc. New York (1972), p. 25.
14. Marlene Fisher, *The Wisdom of the Heart : A Study of the Works of M.R. Anand*, Sterling Pub. P. Ltd., New Delhi (1985), pp. 4-31.
15. C.D. Narsimhaiah, *The Writers Gandhi, University of Punjab, Patiala* (1970), p. 70.
16. Mulk Raj Anand, *An Interview.* 'A Decadent Society Needs Renewal' Daily English ('The Hindu', Sunday, December 11, 1983) (1983), p. 22.
17. Dr. K.R. Rao, *The Fiction of Raja Rao*, Parimal Prakashan, Aurangabad (1980), p. 138.
18. Mulk Raj Anand, *My Experiment with a White Lie,* p. 2.
19. K.R. Srinivas Iyengar, *Indian Writing in English*, Asia Publishing House, Bombay (Fourth Edition), (1984), p. 330.
20. Mulk Raj Anand, *Coolie*, Orient Paperback, New Delhi (1972), p. 317.
21. D. Riemenschneider, *An Ideal of Man in Anand's Fiction*, Indian Literature, Vol. X, No. Jan-March (1967), p. 32.
22. Mulk Raj Anand, *Coolie,* Orient Paperback, New Delhi (1972), pp. 265-66.
23. *Ibid*., p. 264.

24. *Ibid.*, p. 266.
25. *Ibid.*, p. 88.
26. *Ibid.*, p. 188.
27. *Ibid.*, p. 177.
28. *Ibid.*, p. 270.
29. *Ibid.*, p. 260.
30. *Ibid.*, p. 115.
31. C.D. Narsimhaiah, *The Swan and the Eagle*, Indian Institute of Advance Study, Simla (1969), p. 125.
32. S.C. Harrex, *The Fire and the Offerings : The English-Language Novel of India*, Vol. I, Writers Workshop, Calcutta (1977), pp. 97-98.
33. Mulk Raj Anand, *Two Leaves and a Bud,* Arnold-Heinemann Pub., New Delhi (1983), pp. 37-38.
34. *Ibid.*, pp. 193-95.
35. *Ibid.*, pp. 205-206.
36. Dr. G.S.B. Gupta, *Mulk Raj Anand*, Prakash Book Depot, Bareilly (1974), p. 48.
37. Mulk Raj Anand, *Two Leaves and a Bud* (1983), p. 223.
38. Mulk Raj Anand, *Apology for Heroism*, Kutub-Popular, Bombay (1967), p. 74.
39. Mulk Raj Anand, *Two Leaves and a Bud,* Arnold-Heinemann, New Delhi (1983), p. 30.
40. *Ibid.*, p. 123.
41. *Ibid.*, pp. 124-25.
42. S.C. Harrex, *The Fire and the Offering : The English-Language Novel of India*, 1935-1970. Writers Workshop, Calcutta, (1977), p. 105.
43. Jack Lindsay, *The Elephant and the Lotus*, Kutub-Popular, Bombay (1965), p. 9.

3

Beyond the Seas — The Trilogy

Variously described as a 'Marxist Epic', a panoramic vision of pre-war Indian society, an anthropocentric literary exercise, the Lalu Trilogy marks an important phase in Anand's career as a novelist and as a revolutionary idealist. It is perhaps the most ambitious project which he has ever undertaken and embodies his experimental burden as well as his creedal preoccupations, without over-stepping the boundaries of historical humanism, which has been a major obsession with him. Anand delves into the historical past with a view to recrudescing the significant events between 1939 and 1942. The trilogy gives an incisive analysis of the 'tense, fear-ridden, and war-torn world, both in Europe and Asia, out of which these novels were fashioned.'[1] Anand also endeavours shove his personal aspirations and involvements into the narrative pattern such that they acquire the epic amplitude and immensity. Each of the novels retains its separative identity while tending to conform to the narrative continuum by virtue of its projection of the global vision of India. The first novel traces out the development of the protagonist, Lal Singh, from 'innocence' to 'experience' and also successfully renders Anand's indictment on war, poverty, religion and various type of social taboos which afflict the Indian society. Anand successfully blends, in the trilogy, both content and form into the plasticity of his vision and hints at the possible restoration of sanity and wisdom which were perforce lacking in the Indian society. The hagiological saviour, 'the destination man', as Anand prefers to put it, is at the centre of the novels, through the narrative action moves beyond India. The trilogy is also an intense politico-sociological document intended to project a congeries of conflicting forces which impinge on the consciousness of the hero as he gropes for identity. While Anand's protagonists in his earlier fictional experiments like *Untouchable* and *Coolie* become mute witnesses to the diurnal drama of pain and unbridled social mayhem, in the trilogy Lalu comes into the open and reacts sharply to the changing patterns of life and fights valiantly with the ironical forces of a society which tries to intimidate him. He neither succumbs to the rigidities of the caste-system nor kowtows before the sacrosanct religious custom; he is much more bold and venturesome than Anand's earlier heroes like Bakha, Munoo and Gangu since he is cast in an entirely different mould. Lalu is a revolutionary by instinct, and by conscious choice, and he has the nerve to flout all religious and social regimentations which have, according to him, become fetishistic in the ever-changing social context in India. He even becomes a relentless crusader, a dedicated soldier and an arch-revolutionary, gearing up his unbridled strength to galvanise the inarticulate masses into organised incendiarism against all forces of ruthless repressions perpetrated by the *nouveau riche*, landlords and religionists.

The first book of the trilogy, *The Village,* begins with a vivid evocation of the life of the peasants in the Punjab. Born into a traditional family of Sikhs, Lal Singh becomes the very emblem of an anti-hero. His father Nihal Singh is a proud farmer in the village of Nandpur in the Punjab. Lalu quickly reacts to the injustices heaped upon him and wants very much to throw larboard all rigidities of social custom which has seemingly become absolete and anachronistic. He does not see eye to eye with his father's religious observances and meaningless homelities, and keeps himself safely at a distance from the coterie of moneylenders and landlords, whom he considers the stooges of British imperialism. Lalu even goes to the extremity of getting his hair cut in open defiance against the religious ordinations and, in the process, antagonizes the villagers who ostracise him. His adolescent flirtation with Maya, the daughter of the village landlord, lands him into further germinal tensions. Involved in the fabricated charge of theft, and unable to win the whole-hearted support of anybody else in the village, Lalu leaves the village to enlist himself in the 68-Rifles at Ferozpur. He later learns that his brother Sharm Singh has been hanged for murdering the landlord's son, and of his family's involvement in mounting debts. But even amidst the gyrating misfortunes, Lalu is touched by the affection of the villagers when he returns to his ancestral village. He is given a warm send off, later :

> Almost the whole of the village followed him in a procession to see him off the cross-road beyond the carvan serai. It was an imposing procession, marshalled under the tutelage of Kalu, the black dog, who ran along in little capers at the side and occasionally rushed ahead sniffing the trial of some imaginary prey and then tearing back to bark a ferocious farewell.[2]

But further humiliations are in store for him and he is slapped by Lance Naik Lok Nath, a senior military officer, for his minor transgression. He is later taken away from Karachi to an unknown destination and he comes to know of his father's untimely death, and very much desires to come home. He incoherently whispers : 'I will come back to you; but not yet, not for a wife.'[3] The novel thus dramatises the prodigal son's return to the village; to the primal roots, and ends with his eventual departure to an unknown place as a soldier.

Obviously, the novel's plot-construction is weak though it bears the evidence of semi-autobiography which has gone into the making of it, which is now blown out of proportion. Anand no doubt succeeds in evoking the bucolic atmosphere in all its vividness and variegatedness. Apparently it is a transcription of the novelist's felt-experiences, now used in the service of fictional art. As it is, it conveys the intensity and depth of Anand's own ideas and impulses which guided him when he was an adolescent trying to assert his independence and autonomy. Rightly described as an 'Indian pastoral', *The Village* evokes a vivid picture of the Indian rural life :

> As he emerged into the neat, sun-soaked compound, stewn with broken white bubble and smelling of the fresh tar that was painted round the rim of the red-brick building, he halted for a moment to see if any of his sons were there, for usually in the court-yard except the railway porter's wife, who was feeding her chicken with stale lentils.[4]

It is a charming idyll of the Indian rural life, reminisced with a rare fidelity and the facticity. As Alastar Niven points out : 'Several of the themes of the autobiographical novels are re-expressed in *The Village*.'[5] Anand captures, in the vivid cameos of perception the life of Indian peasants, gripped as they are with poverty and continual exploitation, their passions, superstitions, their religiosity and fanaticism, their orthodoxy and genuine intolerance, which readily come to life. To quote Alastair Niven, again :

> Anand's concern is to eradicate poverty and diseases and injustice, essentially practical concerns that need intelligence, worldliness, idealism and certain ruthlessness to become manifest...in *The Village* there is considerable tension produced between his determination to help his people materially...and his regret that in such a determination, there must lie a large gulf between he who wishes to help and those he helps, between the idealist and the object of his ideals.[6]

In writing the modern epic of pain and laceration of the 'have-nots', Anand has chosen the global picture of India, as it emerges from the melee of cultural cross-currents into its own autonomy. It is not so much the story of an individual's struggle against the forces of orthodoxy and regimentation as it is the evocation of a whole saga of vexatious turns and twists induced by the corossive social system which arrests the individual's potential for growth into self-individuation. In writing the trilogy, Anand seems to offer a distant parallelism between his work and that of Stein Beck's *The Grapes of Wrath* and Pearl S. Buck's *Good Earth*. As Jack Lindsay observes :

> He has re-discovered the Indian epical tale in terms of the contemporary struggle. All the while, a continual fusion is going on between the methods of Chatterjee, Tagore, Premchand and the methods which Anand has learned from the study of European novel; and the result is one long experiment in adapting the Indian folk elements to Western eyes and the European elements to Indian

> eyes. In stabilizing and extending the Indian novel, Anand is also adding to the tradition of the novel.[7]

Lalu's cherished ideals and values and his attempts at the conferment of autonomy and social equality on the peasants, are to be further tested and formulated in Europe. The land he has witnessed is not the same, and what Lalu sees is boredom and the horror of death which the Second World War has brought in its wake. His life in the trenches of Cyprus, and in the desolate places of the French countryside, and later in Germany as a prisoner-of-war, form the warp and woof of his next novel, *Across the Black Waters* in which Anand's own experiences of war become transcripted into the creation of one of the finest of war novels in the 'thirties'. As Anand has observed :

> I meant much more than writing a novel of the war. I meant to condemn modern civilization the way it was drifting towards violence and bloodshed and world of pain... (*Across the Black Waters*) is a novel to show the degradation and bestiality produced by merchants of death.[8]

The novel has a conventional plot, with the interaction of character and incident lending to contribute for the narrative progression. It is essentially in the nature of a rambling chronicle, beginning with Lalu's disembarkment at Marseilles and ending with his pathetic plight as a prisoner-of-war at Fostubert. What happens between the two polarising events is the crux of the story. Lalu's confrontation with the war-torn phantasmagoria and his attempts to grapple with the political and social realities and his near-fatidical understanding of life, become the central thematic burden of this novel. Anand charts out the details of the life of soldiers, their anguish and boredom, which they seem to be perpetually condemned to. The novel is thus more concerned with the trenchant facts of life and its attendant horrors and nausea than with a mere social vivisection of the pre-War India. Anand presents the universe which has become atrophied and in which the individual choices are annulled. Even in this foredoomed universe, Lalu seems to experience the *bonhomie* of his fellow men. Lalu's companions die one by one, leaving him disconsolate. Dhanoo is drowned, Lachman Singh is killed in action and Hanuman Singh commits suicide; but in all these shifting processes of change and mutation, Lalu warmly reminisces the comraderie of Kirpu and Lachman, who were too good to him to be easily forgotten. He is more than perturbed to see the horrors perpetuated by war and the sight of the maimed bodies evokes in him an empathy that borders on self-disgust.

> Lalu set coiled up in the slimy straw in the cave, scraping the mud off his boots and clothes. If he had been told even a fortnight ago that in Vilayat, the land of his dreams, where he had been so happy and eager to come as an adventurer, the Sahibs, whom he admired so much, were wilfully destroying each other, ruining their villages and their cities, he would not have believed it.[9]

Concluding his assessment of the novel, S.C. Harrex observes :

> In *Across the Black Waters* sets the natural landscape against a mythic landscape lucid with nightmare sceneries of cosmic destruction and inferno, and in doing so he relies on traditional associations of war with the Indian gods and goddesses of destruction.[10]

Mulk Raj Anand has prepared the rough draft of the novel in Barcelona, Madrid, Spain during the Spanish Civil War in 1937 and has entirely recasted it in England in 1939. As Dr. G.S. Balarama Gupta observes :

> *Across the Black Waters*, in fact, occupies a unique place among Anand's novels, for it is the only novel he has hitherto written exclusively as a condemnation of war and its infernal effects. The characters of the novels are life-like and its incidents have a ring of authenticity, and this is all due to the fact that they all spring from the author's experience, in fact most of the chapters were written actually in trenches.... The novel goes to prove that a work of fiction may achieve much more than what even a powerful tract can achieve.[11]

The novel also deals with the exploitation of the soldiers in the lower rank, in war time, and also exposes the cruelties perpetuated by 'military officialdom'. It is, in fact, an anti-war novel, and is concerned with the exploration of the horrors of war on civilization. As Marlene Fisher observes :

> *Across the Black Waters* operates on at least two levels. On one, it is a powerful, lively, and an indictment of those ills of modern civilization that lead to war. On another, it is the second of that trilogy dealing with 'the life and adventures of Lal Singh'.... Anand has skilfully juxtaposed two levels of content and theme, enlivening his narratives with abundance of vivid details yet preserving their unity by keeping his focus on Lal Singh, and by bringing all threads together in him.[12]

Thus, it is intrinsically a severe indictment on war. The sole purpose of Anand is to show the havoc wrought by war in the life of an individual which blights all hopes of his social betterment. The regimentation of life in the trenches and the progressive ossification of human impulses, human values and the routinized inflexibility which sting the individual's quest for freedom and ordinariness, are all focused with an intensity that is rare in Indian fiction in English, on the one hand, the novel virtually dramatizes 'civilization in violence', and also deals with the pitiless plight of the individuals as they are caught in the maelstrom of conflicting passions and emotional turbulences. On the other hand, it is concerned with the progression of its hero from a seemingly reckless rake to a revolutionary idealist, spearheading the purposive rebellion. Anand seems to show how 'anarchy is loosened upon the world', and explores as to how naivete and primal simplicity of an individual are lost in the war-torn world. Anand largely succeeds in lending to his novel both veracity and authenticity by fusing his own life experiences into the narrative. The two strands of his ideas pertaining to the anti-war indictment and his longing for a millennium of happiness are superbly woven into the narrative tapestry. The novel seems to represent the *finds sickle* nausea that comes at the end of an age. As Riemenschneider points out :

> Life in the army does not change Lalu very much.
> There is little room for his independent working

> out of a concept of life. Lalu is but a particle in the high machinery of the army.[13]

Lalu is one with the millions of the hapless Indian peasantry put under the juggernaut of social custom. In his efforts to bring about a new era of hope and redemption Lalu is 'defeated but not totally vanquished'. He accepts, in the typical Indian tradition, the inevitable, and takes to in his stride the caprices of fate. He accepts, albeit not ungrudingly, his lot as a soldier and drifts into self-isolation and annonymity. The novel thus ends on a note of irremediable cynicism, bordering on disenchantment.

Anand's third novel of the trilogy, *The Sword and the Sickle*, takes its title from William Blake :

> The sword sung on the barren heath;
> The sickle in the fruitful field;
> The sword he sung a song of death.
> But could not make the sickle yield.

The novel presents class-conflict through two prominent motifs of the sickle, representing the vast labour force, and of the sword, symbolising the brute force of imperialistic hegemony. It charts out the return of the protagonist, Lalu, from prisoner-of-war camp in Germany to his native village, with an abundant hope. But his home-coming is none-too-happy, for he finds the country in the grip of post-war depression, and all the attendant horrors of poverty and depradation. He expected that the British Government would reward him suitably, giving him a piece of land in recognition of meritorious services; but his expectations are belied. He becomes demobilised because of his suspected involvement in the seditionist activities, while he was a prisoner in Germany. Humiliated beyond his expectations and bearance, Lalu goes to his ancestral village where further shocks await him. He learns of his mother's untimely death, and his brother Dayal Singh's turning to asceticism. His house and land are auctioned; and there is nothing left to speak of his own or his ancestral connexions. The spirit of desolation pervades the whole story of and Lalu's homecoming. The only solace that he gets is the company of Maya, his one-time beloved and now a widow, who decides to be his wife. Lalu wonders at the rapid gyrations of change wrought by the passage of time. He observes :

> ...What was extraordinary, things were not taken of what they were, as the immutable degree of Fate which no man could alter! Why, there were desperate people forming clubs and bands of bereft. The water was flowing uphill instead of down.[14]

But something different had been happening in the country. A kind of global 'revolution' was in the offing and people became suddenly aware of their inalienable rights. Lalu is fascinated by the proletarian leader, Professor Varma, who talks of retaining self-honour, without compromising with the imperialist Government. Lalu is drawn into the redical socialist group, headed by Kanwar Rampal Singh, the Count, who gathers the like-minded people around him. Lalu is befriended by the Count who takes him to a party thrown by one of the most powerful landlords, who has pronounced sympathies for the exploited. Lalu is thus caught in the contradictory pulls of tradition and modernity and rallies himself with the radical socialists who spearhead a 'revolutionary' movement. In his personal life, Lalu maintains a saintly detachment with Maya, his one-time benefactor. By marrying her, Lalu thinks, he has punished his old enemy, the landlord.

Nonetheless, Lalu remains an unwilling participant in the so-called 'revolution' engineered by Professor Varma* and Kanwar Rampal Singh but later sees the efficacy of the 'Revolution' in bringing about the desired changes. He finds in Mahatma Gandhi,

---

* Anand observes :

"On the return of my hero in *The Sword and the Sickle* you see him deprived of all his land, I then bring him to the decisive area of high landlordism, the talukdars of Oudh. Thus the novel seeks to portray the consciousness of awareness of change in the village, *though man like M.N. Roy who appears in the novel as Professor Varma*. And I show Varma hoping to make Revolution by writing about it. There were communists you know, who thought they could bring about Revolution just by inciting a mob to go and take a police station! Revolution is not just spontaneous revolt, even in Telegana. *So I showed the failure of the Indian revolution at the stage : the failure of intelligentsia; the failure of M.N. Roy and all the others*. The novel thus becomes a tragi-comedy."

(Mulk Raj Anand, 'A Decadant Society Needs Renewal', *The Hindu*, Madras, December 11, 1983.)

a champion of the peasants, and decides to invite him to Raj Garh. But on hearing that he is busy, he drops the idea. He is fascinated by Nehru because he 'is one of us' and moreover 'a socialist',[15] who has pronounced bias for scientific revolution. Lalu's deep-rooted agony, which is characteristically of the novelist's too, is expressed in the following passage :

> This isolation, he knows, was the price he had to pay for abjuring all connections with the false gods of the world, for seeking to speak and act and live by his faith, by the integrity of his knowledge and of the peasant's to the Sarkar which ruled the Indian earth, by becoming an agitator, always on the prowl and in danger of being arrested.[16]

Utterly disillusioned, Lalu prepares himself to participate in the peasants' revolt as it offers him a vicarious satisfaction to quench his idealist's thirst and the novel virtually ends in disillusionment, with Lalu's incarceration. But the novel is not so bleak as it indicates. Lalu receives a telegram from Maya to state that he is blessed with a son. He now knows that the war is a yawning gulf between his former self the present predicament and finds an intimate kinship with the village commune to reconcile himself to the changing patterns of life. He progresses in his self-education and achieves epiphany in his self-certitude. Thus, Lalu's life comes full circle, as it were. Anand largely succeeds in stating, in explicit terms, the accumulated outrage perpetuated by the feudal system against the peasant folk and the horrors of boredom and stupification that they lie in wait. Unlike Bakha and Munoo, who passively accept their pre-ordained roles, Lalu becomes a prophet of revolution by choice and intent, thus signifying the end of an era of uncertainty and the possible new direction which Anand's later heroes take to. Anand himself explains the true purport of the novel thus :

> I have been condemned for writing *The Sword and the Sickle*, I think unfairly, I feel it is...the only kind of third volume of trilogy, I wanted to state there the rise of consciousness and awareness, a new sense of brotherhood.[17]

Anand was attracted to Marxian materialism even in his formative years when he was in England for over two decades in "search of faith", for a viable identity. He prefers to loss his own insecurity in favour of collective good, now that his goals are determined by the basic demands of his profound beliefs and notions. He realises that the human suffering and oppression are unleashed by the forces of imperialism which he detests most. He is trying to spearhead a kind of noble revolution to bring about an egalitarian society. This has been exactly the message of the Lalu trilogy, a fictional fiat which acts both as a catalytic experience and as a vehicle for his propaganda. As Saros Cowasjee points out :

> The Trilogy is an impressive achievement : its scope is epical. It presents a great historical story and it presents it in the fine details, searching out every grain of truth as it goes. Alongwith history, it offers the geography, the folklore, the religion, the values and attitudes of many stratas of Indian society.[18]

In the year 1931, Anand has chanced upon reading Marx's *Letters on India* in which he has found not only a 'a scientific and rational method of a study of society" but also a hypothesis which has led him to new discoveries. Marxism has become a veritable religion for Anand and has opened up many new vistas, and new avenues for channelising his energies. A closer scrutiny of Lalu's trilogy reveals the fact that Anand is nearly on the verge of bringing about a radical revolution, through his protagonist Lalu, whose actions and pronouncements very nearly conform to his proletarian ideology. For Lalu, as for Anand, the word 'Revolution' is as enthralling as any religion and his own experiences had been forcing him to strive for liberating the inarticulate Indian masses under the burden of misery and poverty. Lalu's identification with the peasants' revolution and his endeavours to achieve his goals of social and economic equality and prosperity through revolutionary methods, is well brought out in his candid conversation with Maya :

> I have come to help to convert this prison into free land like Roos (Soviet Russia) where there are no divisions of religion or property among people,

> where women who were sold to the highest bidder, have become free to choose their own lives, where....[19]

His evolution as a radical communist could be traced out the life-cycle of the protagonist as he moves through many undulating processes of change and mutation. Fortunately, he comes under the spell of the Count, Professor Varma, Comrade Sarshar, who whetted his sensibility and gave him all the inspirational philip he needed. In his efforts to bring about the much-needed social change Lalu is not with the establishment; but the methods which Lalu has chosen are as radical and as revolutionary as those of his creator. Anand charts out the progression of his hero from the position of reluctant outsider to an active participant, who now prepares to sacrifice his personal comfort for collective benevolence. The publication of a paper, *Naya Hind* to boost up the morale of the people and his addressing of peasants' rally on the sunlit banks of the Ganges, are all traced out by Anand with a precision that is rare. Lalu, his proletarian messiah, addresses the peasants thus :

> ... today, the gates of a new life will open to you. For, in far off land called Roos (Soviet Russia), too the peasants once suffered as you do, and then they set up their own Raj.... And now the peasants and workers ruling there, and all men there live like brothers.... So give a shout : "All men are brothers!"[20]

There are discussions on 'Community Farming', on private property, on the need for a proletarian struggle for the upholding of the struggle which are all done in the typical mode of 'a committed artist'. In all these events the typical aspects of Anand's own personality looms large;

> Come, let us make another effort to destroy those who do not love us. We failed because, we have not changed, because our habits, ideas, opinions were narrow and contained within the circles of Kisan Nagar. Because neither our leaders nor we ourselves know that all our other brothers were doing — those brothers who have ended up from

> the four corners of India in the mills and factories, escaping from hunger, pestilence and cold into long hours, dirt and disease! We followed the shadow and forget the substance.... Come worthy little people, come, we will now make a real Revolution! Come, we shall work day and night and learn now to make Revolution.... For Revolution is the need of togetherness, comrade, the need to curb malice among men, the need for men to stand together as brothers.... Now it is the time to change the world, to fight for life and happiness — Comrade, sing brave songs of struggle....[21]

The speech is larded with typical words and phrases which are appropriate to or approximate with the revolutionary lagos. Through Lalu's trilogy, Anand seems to visualize "the new dawn filtering through the doorways with that uncanny milk-white radiance which heralds the coming of a strong man".[22] The novel ends with a distinctive note of optimism, and Anand's proletarian odyssey seems to have come full circle. Concluding her assessment of the trilogy, Meenakshi Mukherjee observes :

> The repetition in Anand and his lack of artistic development are symptoms of a basic malady, a malady that is the absence of better term may be described as lack of sustaining myth.... Anand, like his heroes is alienated from a traditional framework of values; while rejecting the superstitions and narrowness, he has also cut himself off from strength-giving continuity of a culture.[23]

There is very little which one can draw from these observations, though she rather provides a cue to understand Anand's conception of an epic of misery, and his preoccupation with the contemporary man's ordeals. Anand distrusts the traditional Indian epics like the *Ramayana* and the *Mahabharata*; he believes that it is no use adopting old myths to the comparatively new form of the novel. He observes :

> I have myself deliberately tried to create and live

> upto a new contemporary myth-man, in his dignity of weakness, struggling to be an individual, a God and of course, failing in the attempt.... I thought, always that a novel is a kind of poem, the 20th century ballad, the folk epic of the new classes, rather formless but immediate in recognition of the quick of life.[24]

The trilogy's epic sweep is to be found in the scale of time, place and events which Anand has set himself to work with. The story significantly begins with 'the birth of renascent nation', and charts out the adventures of Lalu, his eventual conversion into a committed revolutionary. In the first book of the trilogy, *The Village,* Anand describes Lalu's childhood, and his irrepressible instinct to rebel. The novel telescopes the decline of the peasantry, as a result of economic imbalance and poverty and ignorance and superstition which still grip its people. As a sensitive individual, who is caught in the throes of clap-trap tradition, Lalu's story represents the germinal tensions which surface into his rather open defiance of the community's authoritarianism. He rebels against all forms of superstition, and religious sanctions, which is an open affrontory, and thus becomes alienated from the society. In the second novel, *Across the Black Waters,* Lalu is translated into the seething whirlpool of politics of the World War II and lands himself as a prisoner-of-war in Germany. Pitted against the merciless rigours of life in the trenches, Lalu undergoes the turgid purgatorial processes of experience. In the last novel, *The Sword and the Sickle*, Anand traces Lalu's home-coming and his imminent disillusionment. Lalu finds everything so strange and disoriented in the post-War India that he joins the peasants' revolt, and becomes once again a prisoner of conscience. He is exposed to misery and poverty, and is used by wily politicians, who enforce him to throw over-board all his entrenched beliefs and convictions. He comes to know of the disharmony between him and the world; and the trilogy ends significantly not with a sense of abysmal frustration but with a sense of bewilderment and self-catechism. Lalu begins to contemplate :

> What is the destiny of man and how can I control it? Why is it that after a long time of struggle...after

> all effort I made to cure the defects of my nature, going deeper that all my deepest discoveries... after seeking to grapple with my own destiny.... Why is it that I have ended up in the reeking hell....[25]

Mulk Raj Anand observes in his interview :

> The attempt as parallelism of thought and action resulted in the peasant trilogy, *The Village, Across the Black Waters* and *The Sword and the Sickle.* In these novels, I have tried to project my imagination into all these selves...to try and rescue from within their old consciousness come glimmering of hope, beyond imprisoned mind....
>
> The utter decay of India cellular ghetto, groups, families and people of all kinds, was only relieved by new ethic....
>
> The impatience of the two youth to break through the conformism, even to the Gandhian orthodoxy, led to violence inspired by the revolution of the Wast. The rumours of some other cultures destroying the debilitating influence of the restrictive societies elsewhere fairly strong through the heroic sections of men like M.N. Roy, Jawaharlal Nehru and even the old Tagore.
>
> The important thing in these novels of struggle...the failure of spontaneous revolts.[26]

Thus the trilogy, in Anand's own words, is India's 'epic of misery'. It tries to resolve some of the irremediable enigmas of the peasant community, sunk in deprivation and social apathy as it tries to liberate itself into a new awareness such that it could be re-oriented to confront the changing patterns of life and time. Anand suggests, albeit through innuendoes, that the Indian peasantry might emerge into a millennium of freedom, if only it confronts all forces of destabilisation bravely. Lalu's attempts to move towards 'universal humanism' and achieve consonance with the society that has spurned him, and his seeking of distinctive identity as a 'whole man' becomes the structured patterns of the novel. However, the chief burden of Anand's novels, as S.C. Harrex points out, is 'mythic', though one cannot rule out the Marxian overtones. He considers that the first novel of the trilogy *The Village*, is a 'mythopoeic cosmic canopy for the action with ubiquitous influence becomes almost ritualistic at crucial moments'.[27] The intimate relationship of the peasants with the earth and the sky, and various forms of communal observances, lend to the novel a mythic aura. Similarly, in his next novel *Across the Black Waters,* Anand presents the tortuous journey of Lalu into the infernal world of the Second World War, the eventual traumas and lacerations he is made to undergo. Anand describes the nightmarish journey of Lalu, thus :

> A sense of doom was creeping into him, a sense of fear and abject, horror of the dark, unknown forces of this world that weighed heavily on everything even on him who had seen the new things did not believe in superstition of the hosts of dark forces.[28]

Almost in a mood of sombre pessimism, which is akin to that of Hardy's, Anand traces out the evolution of his hero from innocence to experience an evolution, which is social as well as existential. Lalu epitomises the heroic struggle of a modern-day Prometheus caught in his own cultural *hybris*, trying to emerge into a world of consonance and radiance, albeit not without scalding experiences. In his search for meaning and self-sustaining ambience, Lalu is put to a myriad processes of change, ultimately reaching out towards an 'achieved identity', through the contingent agencies of 'the people', 'Revolution', 'Reason' and 'Love'! Lalu's journey 'across the black waters', thus becomes a ritualistic journey of a brave odysseus, questing for a 'new faith', for a new social order. This symbolic journey takes him to different continents, different peoples and different purgatorial experiences. As Anand observes :

> There is a living myth and a dead myth, and the desire image, which is the basis of revolutionary romanticism, must be really creative and must help man to integrate in society and not provide a formula for escape. Poetry must become a kind of courage.[29]

Lalu seems to enact the role of an archetypal hero transisting from an incendiary revolutionary to benign individual, thus achieving a epiphany. Lalu's journey is lone man's 'journey into night' and his quest for a meaningful synthesis culminates in his total identification with the collective revolution. The novel is not all that dark as it is made out; there is still residual hope in the unbuyable integrity of man, in his potential for betterment, and thus, Lalu, the anti-hero, is metamorphosed into a proletarian messiah, into a 'whole man'. Thus, by fusing both this 'poetic realism' and Marxian ideology into the gamuts of his narrative, Anand succeeds in the projection of the 'millenarian myth'. As he observes :

> Though I believe in realism, I am, and I have said for poetic realism. I would like, for instance, to stress the importance of the desire image, or the romantic will, in writing, and I stand altogether for art against literary photography. And just as I found myself insisting in...just as I desired a total and truly human view of experience, a view of whole man, in order that a completely new kind of revolutionary human may arise, so I have been inclined to stress the need for a truly humanist art commensurate with the needs of our time.[30]

Anand's trilogy could also be viewed in terms of his revolutionary idealism, with his protagonist Lalu as 'an Indian Everyman', who embodies in his person the doubts, fears and confused spectacle of millions of Indians in the early twenties. The trilogy is obviously concerned with Lalu's movement from tremulous idealism to a revolutionary diehardism. In the first novel, Anand charts out Lalu's nascent protestations against the rigidities of his caste-system and his flouting of all religious sanctions which initiate him into radical revolutionism. What Lalu experiences in the first novel, *The Village,* is the bitterness of ostracism and his progressive alienation from the society he has loved most.

Lalu's second phase in his evolution is what constitutes the pulp of *Across the Black Waters*. He is drafted into the Army and is taken to Germany, where he becomes incarcerated as prisoner-of-war. The miserable plight of soldiers fighting in the trenches and the utter futility of war reminds one of Ignazio Silone's novel *Bread and Wine*, which Anand is reported to have kept in mind while writing this novel. Anand endorses the view that war is futile since it brings neither glory nor fame to the victorious country. Lalu becomes a prisoner-of-war, but in his consciousness there is something which has moved him very deeply. His revolutionary idealism crystallises only in the last novel *The Sword and the Sickle*, which is described in the words of Frantz Fanon, as the struggle of 'lumpeon-proletariat'. It seeks to project the perpetual struggle and subjugation of the proletariate by the utter cynicism and exploitation of the capitalists. Lalu, after spending his time in Germany as prisoner-of-war, comes back to his village only to find that he has lost his basic connexion with it. He hopes to be rewarded for his services in the British Indian Army, but finds himself a layman, cut off from the life-giving strength and vitality and once again becomes involved in the peasants' struggle, spearheaded by the Count Rampal. But his fighting proves unequal, and he lands himself once again in jail. Thus the trilogy ends on a note of despair born of disillusionment. As Jack Lindsay says :

> In this trilogy then —*The Village, Across the Black Waters, The Sword and the Sickle*, Anand has vividly extended the method with which he begins in *Untouchable*. He has rediscovered the Indian epical tale in terms of the contemporary struggle.[31]

The trilogy is an epic with a difference; here, Anand endeavours to give credence and autochthonous pulsation to his political ideology but fails to objectify his vision. Anand's vision gets blurred by his overenthusiasm to flaunt his ideological passion and humanist sympathies which simply fail to accommodate, Lalu's trilogy would have been a *coda* to Anand's proletarian philosophy had he presented all his ideas through the interaction of character and situation. As it is, Lalu strikes one with angry youngman's posture, flouting all the established social conventions and reminds one of a host of other characters, especially the Black American hero in Ralph Ellison's *The Invisible Man*. As an epic hero, Lalu undergoes different transmutations in his life which culminate in his stoic acceptance of fatality. Though Anand casts him in the role of an archetypal hero, shorn of any great pretensions, Lalu skims out of the novelist's grip and carves out for himself an autonomy and individuality of his own. He is the hero organizing the labourers to revolt against the established order, without caring for the eventualities. He also identifies himself with the masses, and undergoes all the processes of psychic tortures and physical alienation. Though he is aware of the implications of Marxism, he fails to strike a balance between his idealism and social needs. His naivete and earthiness bring him very near to the brink of self-alienation, but he saves himself from slipping into the position of a non-hero. The way in which he participates in the labour organisation, represents a certain historical stage of the emergence of a proletarian messiah. At the end of the trilogy, Lalu is bewildered by the prospects of his rather permanent alienation. He does not find any truth in the words of Professor Varma and the Count; though he has a protracted interview with Gandhiji, he finds in Gandhiji a deliberately exalted simplicity of the egoistical man, talking of self-purification and 'self-perfection'. In Nehru, he finds a more rational man and is more than elated when Nehru promises him to come to the provincial town of Rai Bareli to mollify the emotionally stirred peasants. His self-pride gets dissolved into the general run of politics, and self-honour gets subsumed into the collective mass struggle. This seems to be the real burden of the trilogy, and it does not end with resolvable solutions. As Riemenschneider observes :

> Anand has realized that the individual has first of all to construct in himself a basis for strength of by gaining self-control and that individual man must combine to offer an effective fight.[32]

Thus, the trilogy is redoubtably a propagandistic exercise; it is nonetheless, Anand's most ambitious fictional experiment. He seems to say that the struggle of man for self-realisation lies in the 'communal togetherness', and Lalu's life and traumas to which he is exposed, reveals the fact of his near-achievement of the status of a 'destination man'. As K.N. Sinha observes :

> *The Sword and the Sickle* is expressly a novel of social protest, an emphatic document of peasant life caught in the phase of national regeneration. It seeks to achieve its purpose by dramatizing the class-struggle and by offering social criticism. The

novelist assures full responsibility as guide and mentor. He imposes a moral order upon the multiplicity and non-order of experience. By the same token, the author seems to be committed to a way of life and thinking which has palpable moral design upon the reader. Iyengar has rightly suggested that "Anand the writer of fiction, has necessarily receded to the background."[33]

NOTES

1. Marlene Fisher, *Wisdom of Heart,* Sterling Pub., New Delhi (1985), p. 54.
2. Mulk Raj Anand, *The Village,* Arnold-Heinemann Pub., New Delhi (1984).
3. *Ibid.*
4. *Ibid.*, p. 1.
5. Alastair Niven, *The Yoke of Pity*, Arnold-Heinemann Pub., New Delhi (1978), p. 66.
6. *Ibid.*, p. 67.
7. Jack Lindsay, *The Elephant and the Lotus*, Kutub-Popular, Bombay (1965), p. 25.
8. Marlene Fisher, *The Wisdom of the Heart*, Sterling Pub., New Delhi (1985), p. 63.
9. Mulk Raj Anand, *Across the Black Waters,* Orient Paperbacks, Delhi (1980), p. 119.
10. S.C. Harrex, *The Fire and the Offering*, Writers Workshop, Calcutta.
11. G.S.B. Gupta, *Mulk Raj Anand*, Prakash Book Depot, Bareilly (1977), p. 63.
12. Marlene Fisher, *The Wisdom of the Heart*, Sterling Pub., New Delhi (1985), p. 65.
13. D. Riemenschneider, *An Ideal of Man in M.R. Anand's Novels,* Kutub-Popular, Bombay (1962), p. 39.
14. Mulk Raj Anand, *The Sword and the Sickle*, Arnold-Heinemann, New Delhi (1984), p. 48.
15. *Ibid.*, p. 246.
16. *Ibid.*, p. 344.
17. Marlene Fisher, *The Wisdom of Heart,* Sterling Pub., New Delhi (1985), p. 71.
18. Mulk Raj Anand, *Literaturnaya Gazeta,* November 10, 1948 (In Russian).
19. Mulk Raj Anand, *The Sword and the Sickle*, Arnold-Heinemann, New Delhi (1984), p. 102.
20. *Ibid.*, p. 153.

21. *Ibid.*, pp. 384-85.
22. *Ibid.*, p. 386.
23. M.K. Naik, *Critical Essays on Indian Writing in English* (Dharwar) (1972), p. 231.
24. Saros Cowasjee, *Author to Critics,* Writers Workshop, Calcutta (1973), p. 31.
25. Mulk Raj Anand, *The Sword and the Sickle*, Arnold-Heinemann, New Delhi (1984), p. 388.
26. Atma Ram, *Interviews with Indo-English Writers,* Writers Workshop, New Delhi, pp. 15-16.
27. S.C. Harrex, *The Fire and the Offering,* Vol. I, Writers Workshop, Calcutta (1977), p. 111.
28. Mulk Raj Anand, *Across the Black Waters,* Orient Paperbacks, New Delhi (1980), pp. 206-207.
29. Mulk Raj Anand, *Apology for Heroism*, Kutub-Popular, Bombay (1957), p. 90.
30. *Ibid.*, p. 86.
31. Jack Lindsay, *The Elephant and the Lotus*, Kutub-Popular, Bombay (1965), p. 17.
32. Riemenschneider, *An Ideal of Man in Mulk Raj Anand's Novels*, Kutub-Popular, Bombay, p. 62.
33. K.N. Sinha, *Mulk Raj Anand*, Twayne Publications, Inc. New York (1972), p. 52.

4

The Charmed Labyrinth : Princes and Proletarians

After exploring the agonising plight of the bottom-dogs, in his earlier novels, and their relentless tug-of-war with the implacable, but insurgent, powers of the Indian society in *Untouchable, Coolie, Two Leaves and a Bud*, and Lal Singh's Trilogy, Anand turns his attention to more personal themes, but never overstepping the boundaries of his molecular view of life. The earlier preoccupations seem to have undergone a purposive transvaluation since he skirts the collective to the individual, with the centrality now shifted on the progression of the individual towards self-differentiation. He charts out the course of the hero's movement from bored apathy to one of participation in, and identification with, the fumbling, conglomerate humanity. The two novels, *The Big Heart,* and *Private Life of an Indian Prince* bear evidence of this departure from his rather obsessive preoccupation with ideological Marxian community. The novels under study are magnificently conceived, though Anand fails to fuse various components of his personal life into a cohesive whole. Critical opinion of Anand's later works alternates between unqualified adoration to downright condemnation. Jack Lindsay, for instance, observes :

> If Anand has written nothing else, his place in the history of novel would be secure — his place as profound interpreter of Indian life in the phase of pervasive crisis.[1]

In *The Big Heart* (1945), the story centres round Ananta, a professional coppersmith, who returns to home-town, Amritsar, after doing sundry jobs in factories at Bombay and Ahmedabad.

Having been forced to lead the life of desperation and abject misery, he is driven from pillar to post to eke out his living. He brings with him a tubercular, young widow Janki, and unable to find any suitable job, he settles down to his hereditary work as a coppersmith. He also finds many of the traditional coppersmiths living in deplorable conditions since the introduction of the machine has thrown most of the traditional artisans out of work. Though Ananta hates rapid mechanisation, which aims at replacing skilled artisans, he is not completely against its use. He tells Janki : "like a fashionable vilayati bride we have accepted, we ought to accept the dowry of machine, she has brought!"[2] Realising a pitiful plight of his own kinsmen, Ananta implores the workers to form a Union to bargain with the factory owners for bettering their lot. Mulk Raj Anand makes obvious reference to the global proletarian revolution on the lines of October Revolution in Russia. As he observes :

> There is anarchy and unrest in the world today, but there is every sign that the old life is ending and another new life, is on the way.... We shall give a push to events without our strong shoulders, as they did in Roos (Soviet Russia), for only then we can feed the mouths of the hungry peasants in Hindustan, well, if such pushing and showing brings a certain amount of blood letting we shall stall our hearts and take consolation from the fact that the wars which took many more lives, the greed and selfishness of the rich have caused, took many more lives, out of such a Revolution, brothers, we shall create love and many new things....[3]

Ananta, who is obviously Anand's spokesman, feels the necessity of a change in the social order :

> The legions of men at the end of the horizons were marching in military formations to unknown facts in conflicts a million times bigger than that of Mahabharata in which Pandus and Kurus fought at Kurukshetra.... But his experiences in Bombay through the changes and turns of this titanic struggle has taught him to look at the for Chin

> (Red China) and Roos (Soviet Russia) which had formerly been more rumours to him, lands were rivers of blood had shed by men like himself who had upset the peacock thrones of kings.[4]

Like all proletarian leaders, he belives in 'unity in diversity', and endeavours to bring labourers and skilled artisans under Trade Union as a first step towards collective revolution. He observes :

> In spite, however, of the positive aspect of his belief in Revolution as the only cure for the mismanagement of life by Capitalistis in Vilayat, in Bombay and Ahmedabad, and his belief in the new brotherhood of trade unions which would help to bring about Revolution....[5]

He pleads with the coppersmiths to forge a Union to bargain collectively with the Capitalists, the factory-owwners, and gets the unstinted support of the poet Puran Bhagat Singh. Ananta feels the imperative necessity of 'Revolution'[6] as it is the only binding force in establishing 'brotherhood'[7] and unity. Ananta has already learnt to 'master his destiny with only a big heart'[8] and fraternity of the like-minded people, he feels, alone can spearhead a 'Revolution'.[9]

Anand quotes from the *Gita* : "Krishna said to Arjuna "Live in action"[9] which meant 'fight against falsehood in spite of the odds'. Ananta in his long harangue with his mistress Janki, points out :

> ...a 'Revolution' after which men would find a new brotherhood, away from the pettiness created by the miseries of the present, by the greed of profit makers and the lust of powers of the Sarkar....[10]

The poet Puran Singh, who is virtually the novelists' stooge, joins the tirade against capitalism; he is a man of rare wisdom and infinite compassion, but possessed all the more by the compulsive need for bringing about a proletarian revolution for the betterment. As he observes :

> Never surrender to fear — never never, never.... For if mountains should break and rivers flood and lightings crash, so long as you go on, through weariness, exhaustion and doubt, in the spirit of

> devotion to work and service of others, you will be strengthened that you will go a long way.[11]

It is imperative, he feels, to destroy the illegitimate owners of the workers, the capitalists, who use the machine and the workers for amassing wealth. He seems to say that the destruction of capitalism will lead to the end of greed and alienation, and promises forth the confirmation of a classless society, based on equality and faternity :

> Only a Revolution will complete the reformation and renaissance that is going on among us and produce the new community with new morality in which, and through which men can live creatively.[12]

In fact, Ananta and his sympathisers are "individuals pivotally trying to carry the immense weight of a decadent feudal system corroded with money-oppressions and painfully clinging to ancient forms of thought and action to stave off attack."[13]

Anand's novel, though purportedly deals with the effects of industrialisation on the traditional coppersmiths, it is also concerned with the conflict between the capitalists and labourers. Ananta, another prototype of the proletarian hero, unflaggingly works towards effecting a change in the social order, and bringing about a 'revolution', for which he lays down his life. Though he is 'dead', the hopes of 'revolution' are not blighted at all. As the poet, Puran Singh observes :

> The spirit of his comradeship will survive.... And as nothing that springs from affront and anguish and pain can be destroyed, so nothing must divide those who are left behind to share a common suffering. And the ocean of life will rage again. The tide of love will flow and wipe the waves of hatred.[14]

The novel ends with a bastion of hope and looks forward to a new era of social revolution which purges the society of its evils of discrimination. Discussing the role of Anand, committed as he is to Marxian social order, Mrs. Bald observes :

> Mulk Raj considered capitalism a 'negative kind of revolution (which) did not replace village form it

> destroyed with a better system'. Instead it generated acquisitiveness repulsive to the Indian Intellectual aesthetic and Hindu conscience. Socialism offers an alternative, and Russian Revolution as an example.[15]

Like the preceding novel *The Sword and the Sickle*, the present novel under study is also full of proletarian propaganda, though Anand unsuccessfully tries to conceal it in various fictional artifices. In his task of accommodating the workers thrown out of employment, Ananta gets the unstinted support of the poet, Puran Bhagat Singh, but finds himself unable to muster up sufficient strength to resist rapid industrialisation. He also comes under the influence of Satya Pal, the student leader, who tries to help him out, but things take unsuspected turns when he comes in direct conflict with Ralia, one of the unemployed youths who wantonly destroys the machine in a fit of violent frenzy. In endeavouring to prevent Ralia from his maniacal destruction of machine, Ananta is smashed by him. Ananta sacrifices his own life, fighting to save his own brethren out of ignominy and depredation, thus prefiguring 'humanity's inability to control its environmental fate'.[16]

The Big Heart is one of the most endearing of Anand's novels, for it succeeds, albeit in a limited measure, in projecting the miserable plight of India's "lost generation". Ananta epitomizes all the qualities of a 'big heart', which are not untypical of a hagiological hero. Anand seems to believe that only through traumatic shifts in the fortunes and an exposure to the larger realities of life that man can achieve burnished purity. As Ananta says :

> And I know there will be no more happiness in the darkening world for anyone for long time to come, and I feel I ought to do something before I die so that the others who come after can be a little happier....[17]

Anand reaffirms his faith in human perfectability, and it is by transcending the perversities of life that his character achieves epiphany which is denied to his earlier protagonists. As he observes :

> ...the quality of happiness itself had altered because it has become for him (Ananta) the service of others and the realization of oneself through devotion.[18]

Anand's novel retains the semi-classical dramatic unities as in his first novel *Untouchable.* It has a few episodes and the action is usually confined to a single day. The hero's achieving of martyrdom, not without much laceration, provides the fulcrum for the proletarian drama of class-conflict and self-destruction. The tragic momentum so generated in the main by the destruction of machine by the sectarian intrigues of Ralia who not only destroys the machine but also the generic impulsive of goodness in man. Anand achieves both cohesion and concentration, the tragic emotion so projected crystallising in or metamorphosing into the archetypal conflict between good and evil. Ananta, a modified version of a proletarian hero, meek and unassuming, is destroyed by the preordained forces of environmental fate. In presenting the tragic denouement, Anand depends largely on some anticipatory motifs such as darkness and light which alternate in the narrative action and add symbolic intensity and momentum. Anand writes of his hero in *Apology for Heroism*, has "the big understanding, the generous, the wise heart, informed by passion and schooled by a knowledge born of love".[19]

The story of Ananta is another version of post-lapsarian Adam, 'innocent and rougish', but all the while retaining his moral fortissimo. "There is no talk of money brother, one must have a big heart." He is the archetypal figure who acquires the heroic stature by sacrificing his life for collective good, and in a way he endorses the collective aspiration of his generation by flouting the established norms of the social order. As Jack Lindsay observes :

> This Book...is the most Indian in texture of Anand's writing. It has much of hectic, overstrained element so common in Indian writing the feeling of disproportion somewhere between emotions and their causes, an expressionism which Anand contrasts to realism. But the effect is here intentional use, it is inherent in the situation, in the very texture of the stream of consciousness of the

> people at the particular point of stress in which they find themselves individuals pivotally trying to carry the immense weight of a decadent feudal system corroded with money-oppressions and painfully clinging to ancient forms of thought and action to stave off attack.[20]

And it is significant to note that the novel ends with a note of global revolution which promises forth a new social order whose edifices are built on universalism and social egalitarianism. As S.C. Harrex, rightly observes :

> The sociological idea of tragedy which was formulated in *Coolie* and *Two Leaves and a Bud* is taken a stage further in *The Big Heart*, in which more appropriate literary measures, particularly use of the dramatic unities, achieve great dramatic intensity and coherence.... The poet sees in Ananta the real foundation of the new man. However, it is the poet who articulates the humanism which the hero enacts : I believe in the restoration of man's integrity...the reassertion of man's dignity, reverence for his name and a pure love for man in all his strength and weakness, a limitless compassion for man, and unbounded love especially for the poor and downtrodden....[21]

As in the preceding novels in *The Big Heart*, too, Anand conveys his message of a proletarian 'revolution' through his hagiological hero, Ananta, whose self-sacrifice transcends all barriers of casteism and narrow politics. A closer scrutiny of the novel reveals the fact that it is conceived as a tirade against the feudalistic order which impedes the individual betterment and smothers his inner potential for growth. As Margaret Berry observes : 'In no other novel Anand has attempted to telescope the whole social, economic and political picture'. The problems of caste and class distinctions are so complex that they cannot be viewed isolatively and Anand has dramatized the traditional conflict between the exploiter and exploited in terms of the contemporary fable of an individual defying the feudal hegemony that has corroded the social life. The conflict assumes further piquancy because Anand tries to re-mythicise the struggle of the archetypal hero against the inscrutability of fate. He has made 'the individual typical and typical completely individual'. As Anand further elaborates :

> It is a kind of fable to show how in the whole world you can only conquer the machine now in terms of a new brotherhood.... I say that all these things — machines, politics, parliaments, everything — is to be judged in terms of how it effects the man in his home, the man in his cafe, the man in the train, the man in the telephone booth.... If big dams are made but people can't get water, dams have no meaning.[22]

Thus, the main thrust of the novel is on the class-conflict between the traditional artisans and capitalists, collectively symbolized by the factory owner Murlidhar. The aeons of struggle for collective freedom is also in a way a struggle for proletarian liberalism. Ananta who defies the introduction of machine replacing man, is typecast in the role of a saviour who dies at the altar of the Machine, which is the 'capitalist's stooge and invention'. The task is further taken up by Janki, his mistress who organizes masses into defying the senseless authoritarianism of the exploiters, thus symbolising continuity and renewal of generic human impulsive for revolt. Anand's "destination man" achieves the status of an archetypal hero, a contemporary Promatheus suffering the pangs of rootlessness and bound to a social system that has not yet achieved its insurgency. Anand achieves a tremendous success by fusing into the narrative Dickensian realism and Balzacian passion for the 'illustrational', with a focussed intensity on the environmental forces acting upon this individual's fate. As K.N. Sinha observes :

> The novel is unmistakably his masterpiece. The curve of the plot, the momentum of action, the richness of characterization and the clarity of its moral vision make it an orchestrated whole.[23]

Summing up the true purport of the novel, Alastair Niven points out :

> *The Big Heart*, published in 1945, is saved from economic tract only by the vitality of its central

> character, Ananta, and the dramatic energy of its machine-wrecking climax. The novel is prefaced with a liberal speech made by Lord Byron in the House of Lords on 27th February, 1881, when the Luddities were protesting about the new industrial techniques that were a massive threat to their employment. India's industrial revolution is in the foreground of *The Big Heart*. Though the novel is undoubtedly propagandist, it has a wide and humane scope, surveying the problem — humanitarian, social, cultural, economic, political....[24]

Anand's *Private Life of An Indian Prince*, written in 1948, but published in 1953, is considered to be one of 'the most uncharacteristic of his novels'. It is in the nature of a 'psychotic odyssey' of an Indian Prince, Victor, who undergoes traumatic shifts in his life. There is neither the vehemence of proletarian fury nor the humanist compassion for the bottom-dogs, which had been a major obsession with him. Set against the backdrop of the post-independence era, when the princely states were merged into the Indian Union, the novel is meant to be a "case-study of an individual rather than a historical *dossier*". The central character is Victor, the Crown Prince, who becomes the victim of his own *hubris*. The prince is described as a "spoiled individual, addicted to alcoholism and womanising, a Lawrentian streak which is so uncharacteristic of Anand's heroes. He is obsessed with Ganga Dasi, who paradoxically becomes his Cleopatra, and Beatrice, and who draws him towards venality and self-destruction. The narrator of the story is Dr. Shankar, the Prince's personal physician, who is the 'central intelligence' in the novel. Dr. Shankar has an easy access to the Prince's private life and he plays the Freudian roles of both a narrator and a commentator. His observations, comments and explications constitute, in the main, the story of the novel, and through his fissured consciousness, the private life of the price gets revealed. Intrigue, perfidy, melodrama, intimate observation of the life of the hysterial Prince, his sexual escapades, rife with rumour and scandal — these are all the stock-in-trade techniques of Anand's novel. As Jack Lindsay observes :

> Here is the powerful dialectic of the book, with the

> narrator as the focal point on which the two world of social struggle and the neurotic withdrawal are all impinging. The result is the complex movement of two spirals, one going up and broadening out, the other narrowing down and coming to rest on a point of total collapse.[25]

The story begins with a public scandal in which Vicky, the Crown Prince gets involved. It is rumoured that Vicky, in one of his philandering pursuits, takes Miss Bunti Russell to the ravines to molest her. A case is filed against him which ends in a scuffle with Captain Russell. The Prince becomes scandalized and abused beyond repair, and he indulges in all sorts of wild gestures and vituperative outbursts against the people who try to recriminate him. The narrator tells :

> And now he was hysterical, his voice rising to shrill querulous height, his face livid and tense and contorted into an ugly expression of his lithe bony body like that of viper.[26]

The episode throws a flood of light on the character of the prince as a 'spoilt womaniser', who is on the brink of both personal and political disaster. The Prince is fond of long harangues and exhibits strange histrionics. As the narrator tells :

> For his intelligence seems to have run riot through the large gaps in his education and experience. And this made him pick up many things, with which he was trying to form a single thing but made a bundle of ill-assorted fantansies and facts which incongruous collection into one personally made him a strange, wild creature.[27]

In the next part of the novel, which is in the nature of *denouement,* the significant events of the Prince's life are unfolded, almost with a miniscular precision. Like Lambert Stretcher in Henry James' *Ambassadors*, Dr. Shankar's main function is to see that the Prince is brought to his senses and back to the normality of life to regain the vestigial glory. He finds the Prince in the grip of nymphomaniac mistress Ganga Dasi, who bears him a son. Her sole ambition is to see her son as the heir apparent and her wily machinations are revealed in the course of the narration. Though aware of all her strange antics and histrionics, the Prince becomes powerless to out-manoeuvre Ganga Dasi's designs. To add insult to injury, the Union Government forces him to sign the Instrument of Accession, which Vicky promptly refuses. But the public resentment mounts up and the private life of the Prince no longer remains private. And when he finds that he has no other option left than to accept the proposal of Sardar Patel to surrender his princely state to the Indian Union, he loses both his State and his wisdom and becomes a virtual psychopath. As the narrator tells :

> And while he suffered the agonies of hell from the up and down of Gangi's incalculable temperament, he was fascinated by the challenges of her moods, by the excitement and thrills of those changing colours, of which her vanities, frail ties, ficklenesses and cruelties were the secondary hues as against the lush splendour to the colours of her lusts and passions.[28]

The last part of the novel deals with Vicky's translation into the lunatic asylum, his protracted exile in London and the collapse of his mental powers. Though he has had Lawrentian love-life with the shop-girl, June Withers, Vicky is still possessed by the passion for Ganga Dasi, his one-time mistress. After having lost both his princely State and Ganga Dasi, Vicky virtually slips into dementia, like Lear.

> I am Maharaja Ashok Kumar of Sham Pur. Don't you understand, you swine! I am a Prince! Why, why do hold me like that? Let me go, Let me go, rape-mother![29]

Anand once observed that the novel was written 'in a month and half' in 1948. One can discern a remarkable proximity between the life of the novelist and that of his character, though Anand has rightly warned us that the resemblance with the *persona* is merely gratuitous. In fact, the novel is much more than this; the whole view of the pre-independence era comes readily to one's view. In the character delineation of Dr. Shankar, Anand not only finds an interesting character but also a skilled recounteur in whose spool of thought are unwound the significant historical events. As Dr. Shankar comments :

> In a way the whole of India was a kind of lunatic asylum...in which only those who struggled against the *status quo* and gave battle to authority seemed to find some sense of balance through the elaboration of new sense of values.[30]

He is also the mouth-piece of the novelist, who feels that only through an organised revolution and not meekly submitting to time-tested principles of religion that India can come out of the social morass it has sunk into. Dr. Shankar rightly anticipated global social revolution in India. As he observes :

> ...that young, rising on the curves of their hopes for a better life for vast section of wretched humanity, were prone to turn their backs on superstition, black magic, spiritualism and embraces such libertarian ideas as had been prompted by great European thinkers from Voltaire and Dierot and Bentham and Mill and Spencer and Comte to Marx.[31]

Dr. Shankar rightly anticipates revolution in India, which is the only way out for ending the age-old antagonism between the rich and the poor. He knows fully well that freedom presupposes the abolition of all kinds of barriers. The Indian society, based on the traditional stratification, needs a thorough re-orientation in the form of a revolution on the lines of French and Russian revolutions :

> This change has come from the steady movement of mankind from the age of pre-history to our modern times...hastened by the French and the Russian Revolutions...liberty and democracy and man's relation to religion, and the new knowledge — there has been arising a man, a new kind of human being....[32]

Dr. Shankar is out and out a communist and his affluence has not made him indifferent to the suffering humanity. Dr. Shankar observes :

> ...he was no sure I was a Red.
> I confessed perhaps I was.[33]

Dr. Shankar is not only a personal physician but also a narrator in the novel. He is in fact a spokesman for all Anand's humanist ideals. It appears that Anand, through his character, endorses his ideas about a global revolution of the sort he anticipates in India. As he observes :

> If you look at the history of the last two thousands years the Russians have never attacked India. It was Huns, the Mongols, the Turks, the Tartars, the Portuguese, the Dutch, the French or the British, but never the Russians.[34]

This novel was written after the end of the Second World War. Anand believed that the model of the October Revolution in Russia, would extricate India from the present predicament of uncertainty. As Dr. Shankar, his spokesman observes :

> And there was confusion all around, except in Russia, where Lenin and Bolsheviks upturned the Czarist Empire and, wiping out much feudal decay, began an experiment in a new kind of community living, in which men were to be united.[35]

Analysing the turbulent situation of the State of Sham Pur, where the people reeled under the feudalist oligarchy, Dr. Shankar comes to the conclusion that a total revolution as of the Bolsheviks alone can salvage India from the miasma and moribund social values which have obviously become irrelevant.

> For impinging on my consciousness was the pressure of the people of Sham Pur...lying in the waste wait to ambush and intriguing, agonized, decadent prince and his courtiers and ready to wipe out the whole putrescent order with a ruthless determination to clean up Augean stable of the feudalist oligarchy.[36]

Dr. Shankar believes in the liberal doctrines as doled out to him by the Communists. As a staunch believer in Marxism, Dr. Shankar wants that all distinctions be wiped out, and if it needs be, the old set-up be destroyed so that a new society, purged off all its social anathemas, emerges. He says :

> It seem that the Sardars fall out with the Communists, because the guerillas began to divide up the land among the peasants on the estate of these noblemen...the communists and the peasants keep shifting and go to other villages, divide up the land there, leave a small commune behind and go further a field.[37]

Dr. Shankar rightly feels that the proposal put forward by Sardar Patel and the Accession Bill that was passed in the Parliament with a view to annexing the Princely States of the Indian Union is needless; instead he wants the communists to take over, for the security proffered by the Communist dictatorial regime is more tolerable than democratic liberalism. In fact Dr. Shankar opines that India should come out of feudal-cum-bourgeois constraints by delinking itself from the traditional mores and customs to be able to confront the new realities of life.

> I could have no hopes of changing Victor of Gangi or the state of affairs of Sham Pur, unless I could go out and help to smash the whole fabric of this feudal-cum-bourgeois society and get together with people who wanted to rebuild it.[38]

Like his creator, Shankar has witnessed the immitigable misery and poverty afflicting the Indian masses, and feels the exigency of effecting a total transmutation in the social order. He graphically presents the miserable plight of the Indian 'have-nots' thus :

> A cursory glance revealed the miserable condition of humanity in the narrow, confined little thatched cottages, as skeleton after skeleton showed up.[39]

Private Life of an Indian Prince is a "a Dostoevyskian novel on the grand scale", dealing purportedly with the decadent feudal system, corroded by money oppression. Anand is as much concerned with a 'phase of pervasive crisis' in the conglomerate society as he is with the individual, with the 'montage-man', a pathetic creature and a spoilt child'. Anand is preoccupied rather overbearingly with the character of Vicky for, in him, he finds a kind of remote semblance of a man ruined not by the outward circumstances but the cultural *hybris*. As Anand observes :

> For here was a prince who has been educated in the English Public School tradition and yet whose home background encouraged the darkest superstitions and the most obscurantist ideas. The most barbaric impulses of both civilizations dominated him and he played fast and lose with life without asking himself any questions about himself.[40]

Anand presented Vicky as a romantic hedonist, a libertine in his own right. His upbringing is none too happy and he develops a peculiar streak of narcissism and megalomania. He is terribly unbalanced and is over-powered by irrational *oeuvre*. A pervasive sense of rootlessness or alienation bedims his vision and his rational faculties. He is, in short, a relic of the decadent society, a helpless creature caught in the throes of conflicting circumstances, on the verge of undergoing several brain-storms, like Lear. He mutters :

> The trouble is that I am a genius whom nobody understands! But I shall make you understand! I shall make everyone understand! I shall show you the stuff I am of! I... I... I....[41]

He is a romantic idealist who does not see beyond his nose, and a masochist who becomes the victim of irremediable venalities. His excess self-centredness makes him morally infirm and culpable though he possesses a 'big heart'. Motivated by oedipal passion, he loses his sense of rationality and fails to extricate himself from the 'calamitous carnal obsessions'. Vicky is merely a passive witness to the decadent social order which has lost its moorings. Trapped in the psychotic nightmare, he becomes a pathetic individual indulging in all acts of 'Empodoclean self-destruction'.

In fact, there is much of Byronic intensity in his transition from life-sustaining *oeuvre* to a kind of psychotic journey of self-destruction. As Cowasjee points out there is much of Anand in the character of the prince. As he observes :

> There is as much of Anand in his Prince as in his narrator, and this is partly accounts for the

> penetrating psycho-analysis of the Prince's character. Dr. Shankar is the rational side of the author analysing the irrational side as seen in the Prince.[42]

Another interesting character is Ganga Dasi, a hill-woman. She is the daughter of priest, Pandit Piare Lal, and her mother is a whore. 'Ganga Dasi is attached to her mother' and several of the village herdsmen had her in the hill before she was fourteen. She becomes addicted to the bohemian pleasure-seeking and matures beyond her years. When she meets Vicky, she tells him 'all the secrets of her affairs' and wishes that 'she had met him when she was nearly a virgin'. She had a love experience even before she has met Vicky. Vicky knows that she is a bitch more interested in self-pampering than in genuine love. As Vicky observes :

> I like to sleep with her. I am trapped... I am like rat in a hole... she wants other men. Even while I am having her, she is often telling me of the sexual feats of my cousin Raghbir Singh or someone else. She has never been satiated although she has had so many men.[43]

Vicky knows that Ganga Dasi 'is a consummate actress' and has had a dalliance with numerous suitors. She is a veritable Moll Flaunder given to venality and profligacy.

> And the whole of our life together has been poisoned by my fists of jealousy and Gangi's inability to suppress the harlot in her.[44]

Victor is possessed by Ganga Dasi and in return he desires that she should possess him. Like the Lawrentian hero, he moves from one woman to another, but fails to overcome his passion for Ganga Dasi.

> A compulsion to conquer the members of the opposite sex and to change lovers dominates the nymphomanic. And yet, as most men and women exhibit the same traits to some extent, no one noticed that she was a schizoid or split personality.[45]

Ganga Dasi plays a vital role in the life of Vicky, who himself is a notorious philanderer. Vicky neglects everything, and prepares to surrender before Ganga Dasi's sexual prowess.

> And how was one to measure the span through which she had come to despise him and yet have him constantly in mind? Did the secret lie in the undermost, entangled root of sex, the concealed source of many things, which one never sees ?[46]

Vicky knows the 'language' of her 'body' and falls a victim to her machination. He seems to be attracted to her as a moth by the fire. He says :

> I have come to one conclusion about woman : that they prefer bad men. When I was a wild youngman, I could have had any woman for the asking.... I feel that they are fascinated by evil.[47]

Vicky knows fully well that Ganga Dasi's escapades, and her relationship with Kurt. But still Vicky pines for her :

> She is whore but I want her. I need to put my arms around her to feel safe. I shall go mad if she does not come![48]

The greatest weakness in Vicky is Ganga Dasi, who paradoxically becomes the agent of his ruination :

> I can't rest without her. I need a woman. And she is the woman. I need her support. What with all the troubles of the state I need her by me now especially.[49]

Ironically enough, Vicky does not understand Ganga Dasi, while Dr. Shankar has a complete understanding of her prowess and her spell on Vicky. Dr. Shankar rightly observes :

> I think, that she wants ultimately to be one her own, and alone, away from all the men who foul her, taking them and the other she needs and thus be active in life, but not to be absorbed by them. But what you are seeking is absorption with her. And this she resists, because she does not really want to be possessed, even though she wants to possess. It is this conflict in her, between being

> possessed and dominated and the will to be free, that makes thing different. She wants to run wild like a goat, from mountain to mountain, while a strange ambition to get there, she does not know where.[50]

Mulk Raj Anand has returned to India in 1945 to settle down in Bombay. He very much wanted to bring his English wife, Kathleen Van Gelder, and his daughter Rajini with him. In Bombay a chance meeting with a clever Ceylonese Hill-woman Silva, initiates him into bohemian life. Miss Silva is a talented woman whom Anand has loved most. In 1948, he returns to England to obtain divorce from his former wife so that he could marry Silva. After obtaining legal divorce from his first wife he came back to Bombay. But curiously enough Miss Silva has fallen in love with a Frenchman and has already left for Paris after the marriage. Eventually Anand suffers a nervous breakdown and is nourished by a Greek dancer, on whose advice he is said to have written *Private Life of An Indian Prince*. As Saros Cowasjee further observes :

> Ganga Dasi has her origin in the hillwoman who initiated Anand's divorce. Maharani Indira bears some relation to Kathleen Van Gelder. Anand used to tell her, 'If I were dying, I am sure, sure you would come to nurse me.' In the novel Maharani Indira goes to look after her husband when he has been admitted to the asylum.[51]

Anand has written the novel mainly "to achieve a personal catharsis through the creation of a hero broken by the destructive force of love". Hence the clinical analysis of the character of the Prince who replicates his own life-story. Since Dr. Shankar, who is verily the Conradian narrator, has the intimate knowledge to the inaccessible secrets of the Prince, he is eminently fitted to narrate the insidious story. Dr. Shankar charts out the painful processes of the Prince's psychotic journey, his landing in lunatic asylum and his ultimate ruination, without any trace of sentimentality or overt simplification. When the Prince is landed in lunatic asylum, Dr. Shankar nurses him to normalcy and undergoes with him all the painful processes of change and mutation. But all the way, he remains a detached observer, albeit perceiving the progressive disintegration of the Prince with pain and concern. Dr. Shankar is the veritable sounding-board for all Anand's proletarian values and serves as a connecting link between the aristocratic order and modernising principles of socialism. As Jack Lindsay observes :

> There is a complicated fusion of old and new of medieval and bourgeois elements, of ancient tribal survivals with their strong communal outlook in village life and the first stirrings of social consciousness; history has conspired to produce a hurly-burly of engrossing interest-diversity, humour, pathos, agony and heroism. The obstructive forces and compounded of high antiquity and of uptodate bureaucratic corruption or incompetence. Hence the new method of *The Private Life of an Indian Prince* in which the earlier ironic elements are brought to a head, detached, strengthened afresh with a sense of pathos and compassion. The extraordinary contradiction of Indian life are adduced with a clear-eyed humour with at the same time strays into mere derision; a deep sympathy, impish and yet solidly based on an unfailing sense of common humanity, pervades all the lucid ironies and its moral judgements.[52]

In fact, he becomes the recorder of all the cherished ideals of the novelist as hinted at in his *Apology for Heroism,* though Anand is at pains to explain that the ideas and utterances of his character should not be construed as his own. He observes :

> The neutral 'I' of the first person singular has tended in this book, to become a character in his own right. Most writers know how a character in a novel sometimes takes control and runs away with the story.... Therefore, the 'I' in this novel is not to mistaken for the author, who has reverted to the Indian tradition of anonimity and looks on, like Siva's searing Third eye, at the unfolding of this tragi-comedy.[53]

Thus, the novel represents not only the disillusionment of a single individual who is caught in the labyrinthine recesses of passion and megalomania but also assumes the veneer of a historical chronicle tracing out the slow degeneration of the bourgeoise culture and emergence of a new social order. While Victor symbolizes both vanity and venality, Dr. Shankar represents wisdom and rationality in a world bereft of moral fibre. It is basically a story dealing with the process of disintegration, both personal and collective, and it is odious to describe it 'as a titillating exercise of sensationalism', as a few critics would describe.

It is a well-conceived novel with 'a real political element' and testifies to Anand's ability at achieving a transmutation of his felt-experiences into a veritable historical *dossier.* As K.N. Sinha rightly observes :

> ... a study of human personality caught in the labyrinth of passion, it is eminently successful.[54]

NOTES

1. Mulk Raj Anand, *The Elephant and the Lotus,* Kutub-Popular, Bombay (1965), pp. 27-28.
2. Mulk Raj Anand, *The Big Heart*, Arnold-Heinemann, New Delhi (1980), p. 31.
3. *Ibid.*, pp. 202-203.
4. *Ibid.*, p. 67.
5. *Ibid.*, p. 119.
6. *Ibid.*, p. 89.
7. *Ibid.*, p. 138.
8. *Ibid.*, p. 138.
9. *Ibid.*, p. 175.
10. *Ibid.*, p. 176.
11. Mulk Raj Anand, *The Big Heart*, Arnold-Heinemann, New Delhi (1980), p. 69.
12. *Ibid.*, pp. 143-44.
13. Jack Lindsay, *The Elephant and the Lotus*, Kutub-Popular, Bombay (1965), p. 20.
14. Mulk Raj Anand, *The Big Heart,* Arnold-Heinemann, New Delhi (1980), p. 230.
15. S.R. Bald, *Novelists and Political Consciousness,* Chanakya Publication, Delhi (1982), pp. 132-33.

16. S.C. Harrex, *The Fire and the Offerings,* Vol. I, The Writers Workshop, Calcutta (1977), p. 124.
17. Mulk Raj Anand, *The Big Heart*, Arnold-Heinemann, New Delhi (1980), p. 136.
18. *Ibid.*, p. 137.
19. Mulk Raj Anand, *Apology for Heroism*, Kutub-Popular, Bombay (1957), p. 107.
20. Mulk Raj Anand, *The Big Heart*, Arnold-Heinemann, New Delhi (1980), p. 11.
21. Lindsay Jack, *The Elephant and the Lotus*, Kutub-Popular, Bombay (1967), p. 20.
22. S.C. Harrex, *The Fire and the Offering*, The Writers Workshop, Calcutta (1977), pp. 124-27.
23. *Ibid.*, p. 79.
24. K.N. Sinha, *Mulk Raj Anand,* Twayne Pub., Inc. New York (1972), p. 58.
25. Alastair Niven, *The Yoke of Pity*, Arnold-Heinemann (1978), New Delhi, p. 81.
26. Jack Lindsay, *The Elephant and the Lotus*, Kutub-Popular, Bombay (1965), p. 27.
27. Mulk Raj Anand, *Private Life of an Indian Prince,* Arnold-Heinemann, New Delhi (1988), p. 37.
28. *Ibid.*, p. 46.
29. *Ibid.*, pp. 86-87.
30. *Ibid.*, p. 334.
31. *Ibid.*, p. 340.
32. *Ibid.*, p. 347.
33. *Ibid.*, pp. 246-47.
34. *Ibid.*, p. 207.
35. *Ibid.*, p. 210.
36. *Ibid.,* p. 268.
37. *Ibid.*, p. 207.
38. *Ibid.*, p. 219.
39. *Ibid.*, p. 123.
40. *Ibid.*, p. 176.
41. Mulk Raj Anand, *Private Life of an Indian Prince,* Arnold-Heinemann, New Delhi (1983), p. 69.
42. *Ibid.*, p. 100.
43. Saros Cowasjee, *So Many Freedoms,* Oxford University Press, New Delhi, p. 56.

44. *Ibid.*, p. 78.
45. *Ibid.*, p. 85.
46. *Ibid.*, p. 144.
47. *Ibid.*, p. 141.
48. *Ibid.*, p. 319.
49. *Ibid.*, p. 276.
50. *Ibid.*, pp. 148-49.
51. *Ibid.*, p. 191.
52. Mulk Raj Anand, *Private Life of an Indian Prince, Introduction,* Arnold-Heinemann, New Delhi (1983), p. 19.
53. Jack Lindsay, *The Elephant and the Lotus*, Kutub-Popular, Bombay (1965), pp. 26-27.
54. Mulk Raj Anand, *Private Life of an Indian Prince, Author's Note*, Arnold-Heinemann, New Delhi (1983), p. 23.
55. K.N. Sinha, *Mulk Raj Anand,* Twayne Pub., New York (1972), p. 66.

5

From Realism to Myth : Short Novels

Anand's literary career seems to have undergone many undulating processes of change and mutation, though his outlook on life and his humanistic concerns remain the same. He came back to India from his self-imposed exile in England with a view to permanently settle down in Bombay in repose and in contentment, but all the more sizzling with the same kind of buoyancy, which guided him all through. After India's achievement of Independence in 1947, it appears that Anand's righteous indignation for 'India's lost generation' and his concern for "man's inhumanity to man" seem to have lost their edge and pointedness. With the disappearance of the British composite 'enemy', symbolising the colonial hegemony, Anand appears to have been left virtually with no fictional ambience. He had written *Private Life of an Indian Prince* with an intention to 'cure' himself of several anathemas and the novel seems to have attracted very little critical attention, though it is powerful in parts. Now, Anand has comparatively eased himself of the reformist zeal, which has been a major obsession with him and has turned his attention to remythicise contemporary reality. But curiously, excepting the first short novel, *The Old Woman and the Cow*, the other narratives are deficient in *gravitas* and lack the sustained vital of myth. The reason why Anand has chosen the mythical framework in preference to the centralising theme of proletarian protest, which punctuated all his earlier novels, is not far to seek. Anand seems to have felt, as does James Joyce, a vicarious interest in myth and the need for turning to ancient Indian culture. These are all non-political themes, in which Anand tries to telescope the plight of the Indian woman's or man's gruelling toils and pains, and his or her graduation to self-differentiation. In the first novel *The Old Woman and the Cow,* Anand seems to have purposively grafted the Indian myth, a new mode which perhaps better suited to his artistic needs, in the changed perspective. He grafted the central myth of the *Ramayana* to *The Old Woman and the Cow* (sub-titled as '*Gauri*'). But in adopting the ancient myth to a purely contemporary setting, Anand seems to have become embroiled in insurmountable difficulties. The story of Sita and her abduction by Ravana, her undergoing the ordeal by fire and her ultimate merger with the elemental mother-earth, are all familiar to the Indian readers. Anand endeavours to give the old myth "a new habitation", but in his over-enthusiasm to see that the myth bends to his artistic needs, he makes it jejune and unconvincing. R.K. Narayan, when juxtaposed with Anand, succeeds very largely in adopting the myth of Bhasmasura to his story in *The Man Eater of Malgudi*, which not only sustains the tempo of the traditional myth, but also enhaloes it in symbolic mould.

In Gauri, who is married to Panchi, a man 'with feet of clay', one finds a docile and non-committal wife, who is pre-destined to suffer the worst forms of humiliation. Put to gruelling household tasks and carrying with her the stigma of an inauspicious presence, Gauri virtually finds herself 'unhoused' and alienated. She is even abused and beaten up by her husband for all her unconscious transgressions. She is ill-treated by her mother-in-law, and even her chastity is questioned. Unable to bear the constant nagging of her mother-in-law, she returns to her village of Piplan only to be sold by her mother, Laxmi, to Seth Jairam Das, a banker in Hoshiarpur 'in lieu of cash and the wiping out of the mortgaged two houses as well as a Cow, Chandari.'[1]

Thus, Gauri's home-coming is none too happy. Sold to a man without the qualms of conscience, she resists the amorous advances of the banker and seeks refuge in a nursing home of Colonel Mahindra, a sensitive and upright doctor, who gives her both shelter and consolation. But even there, she has had to fight out the attempted molestation by Mahindra's co-partner Dr. Ratan Chand Batra. Nonetheless, she exhibits a remarkable forbearance and makes her living bearable under the protective tutelage of Dr. Mahindra. At the end, Gauri is restored to her husband through the now-repentant mother. Her husband is glad to have her back, but wants to test her chastity. Gauri finds that the whole situation has gone berserk, and protests with the resoluteness not unbecoming of her characteristic moral compunction and heroic fortissimo. She says :

> "I am not Sita that the earth will open and swallow me" and "takes the road back to Hoshiarpur to begin her life anew."[2]

The novel is dedicated to Ali Sardar Jafri, an eminent, Marxist Urdu poet, and one of the poineers of the 'Progressive Movement' in Urdu. In the dedicatory note Anand says :

> The story of *The Old Woman and the Cow* has been narrated here from the urge to retell in my own manner. The spark that lit the ire that has raged in the book comes from your heart, many years after Nekrassov had left the smouldering ashes of his epic poem in me.[3]

The novel has been inspired by a reading of *The Peasant Woman*, an epic written by the 19th century Russian poet, Nicholas Nekrassov. Anand observes :

> ...the theme of my novel was just conceived after reading...the third part of the great poem entitled : *The Peasant Woman*, many years ago. If my book is sad, like its prototype, then it is not because I don't see hope, but because I am conscious of the present despair.[4]

In the epilogue, Anand quotes from the epic which says "God himself has lost the keys of welfare and freedom of women...[5]* 'who hurls defiance at religion, authority, society, state, tradition, suffer banishment like Gauri....'[6] Colonel Mahindra, like another of

---

* Anand says : "Sita myth doesn't apply.... She is condemned to death. And she burns herself.... I think it is not the lot of woman to become Sita any more.... Woman in our society has been so much humiliated that there is no way by which you can restore her dignity, except by rejecting the Ramayana myth, as I have done in Gauri....

("A decadent Society Needs Renewal", *The Hindu*, Madras, dated 11-12-1983, p. 22.)

his fictional counterpart, Dr. Johan de la Havre, endorses the novelist's proletarian views. In this character delineation, Anand seems to have paid less attention, excepting Gauri, who is the central character in the novel and around whom much of the narration revolves; the other subsidiary characters have not been paid due attention. But in the development of character such as Colonel Mahindra, who appears to be the replica of Dr. John de la Havre, Anand finds his mouth-piece. Colonel Mahindra is also obsessed with the evolutionary idealism as, all Anand's other protagonists. Colonel Mahindra observes :

> ...I am not blaming you. I am blaming your dharma — according to Jawala Prasad you are immoral if you do not pay the interest on debt. To be sure, these hypocrites and the priests are together.... In our village in Gurgaon, the pure, pure Hindus have turned out all the untouchables. And this happens in Gandhi raj. All those dhotiwallas pronouncing half truths! Partial prophets! Compromising! Compromising with the big Seths while the people are helpless.... It is socialism or nothing![7]

Colonel Mahindra also has plans of bringing about a radical social change and is prepared to do anything to infuse both sanity and wisdom among the people who are still gripped by superstition and orthodoxy. In his relentless fight with *status quoism*, Dr. Mahindra tries to educate the people on the principles of equality and oneness. He detests money-power of the capitalists and resents their methods of repression and exploitation.

> All life in our country today, everything in it has been poisoned by the importance given to money, property and possession!.... First there were the white sahibs and now there are the brown sahibs. The banias are hoarding food-grains while the people are dying. And for one good man at the head there are millions of self-seekers.[8]

Dr. Mahindra longs for fraternity, envisages complete happiness and tries to ensure an era of social equality. He observes :

> We must end the cycle of poverty and death. The world died several times because men would not heed the dangers before them.... We have to use our instruments and machines wisely, when the old dark ages are ending and new ages are beginning. Our people, long oppressed by Ferungis, are free. Now we have to dedicate ourselves like bhaktas, to Bharat Mata and humanity. And we have to struggle to build life, to work, and work, so that everyone can eat. There is a wretchedness beyond wretchedness in our land, the most terrible squalor. Our people have been living like the denizens of hell. Twisted, tormented by blood sucking Rakshas! Perverted!... We must build the new life....[9]

Dr. Mahindra believes that '...the salvation of men, requires socialism and not the profit system....'[10] He is equally against the religious practises, which he feels are the bane of the Indian society; words like theism and religion sound frivolous and irrelevant in the changing context of modern life. He ironically pooh poohs all the traditional modes of orthodoxy and regimentation. As he observes :

> They will consider me an atheist, an irreligious, wanton sahib, spoiled by the life in Vilayat!... And they will not easily give up their religion and their servility to new god of money. They will change in time when the great upturning ploughs up their lives and renews the earth. The direction in which we are going is good. But there will have to come young men and women who will take vows of dedication, who will be like Easai missionaries who go into the wilds and serve the lepers. But you folk must hang on to your turbans![11]

He is sorely disgusted with the state of affairs in India and foresees little change for the better in near future. Panchi, another of Anand's characters, puts forward a fatalist's views 'The Gods are dead and we are living dead in this dying world....'[12]

Panchi is another version of an Indian peasant, in whom robust optimism gets devitalised in the face of environmental pulls. He seems to replicate the mythical archetype Rama, who is swayed more by the moral justice than by clear-headed rationality. Anand has, therefore, inverted the myth of the *Ramayana* to suit the contemporary notation, and this seems to be the logic behind his grafting of the old myth to the 'new recital form'. Anand has further observed :

> To me creative writing becomes an expression of life, and not beautiful prose for its sake.... I would no longer live by the dead ideas of traditional philosophies, the rituals of the old religions, or by the tame words of the classics. I would break all forms to try and create new formless forms.[13]

In fact, Anand's revolutionary use of technique is one of negation, and not of affirmation, of the Sita myth. He seems to say that it has become stilted because of the overuse. Many critics have lauded Anand's venturing into the mythical mode, particularly his handling of the theme in *The Old Woman and the Cow*, to suit his contemporary needs. As Premila Paul observes :

> *The Old Woman and the Cow* is the only novel in which Anand spins the plot around a woman character, Gauri, the heroine, falls in line with Anand's suppressed heroes. But while most of his heroes register their protest within the framework of evil society, Gauri sheds her narrow domestic coils before they can strangle her to death, and escapes into the refreshing world of modernity. Whereas most of the heroes face premature death, she emerges as an awakened woman, with a fresh lease of life.[14]

Anand has stressed in his "Old Myth-New Myth : Recital Versus Novel", the need for effecting a synthesis between tradition and modernity in novel form. He is conscious of the hazards involved in keeping up the spirit of the old myth sustained in the contemporary idiom. In his endeavours to delineate the character of Sita in the *persona* of Gauri, Anand partly succeeds in making her essentially human, naive and lovable; where exactly he fails is in the development of the subsidiary characters. For example, in the character delineation of Panchi, Anand attempts to show the predicament of an individual unwittingly caught betwixt the psychological pulls and social demands which overweigh his conscience. Panchi is apparently an unheroic hero, a cardboard figure without any individuality of his own, while Gauri is "cow-like" in her goodness and keeps up her essential naivete and purity of character so characteristic of an Indian woman. Instead of meekly submitting to the irrational demands of society, she takes the road to Hoshiarpur, which is both a redemption from the inflexible social custom and age-old bondage from male chauvinism. Gauri's character is drawn with expert strokes and her gradual initiation into defying the customary male-domination is as indeed an act of self-assertion. As Anand observes :

> Gauri who believed in the worship of her lord and master and wanted ultimately to conquer him with her devotion...and willing to wait like the Hindu wife and go patiently through everything.[15]

Like Hardy's *Tess*, she has now abandoned the Gods of her religion, and readies herself to confront the malevolent fate. Her "Doll's House" now crumbled, she turns her back on the society which has spurned her, exactly in the manner of Nora in *A Doll's House*. As S.C. Harrex observes :

> The novel might be called his pastoral version of poetic realism.... The story conceived as a folk tale of modern India. The plot is uncomplicated. An archetypal situation sets the narrative in motion. The main action of the novel concerns the heroine's travails and it develops conventionally, fluctuation from catastrophe to survival in accordance, as it were, with the inevitable laws of dharma.[16]

Thus, Anand's novel *The Old Woman and the Cow* is a powerful evocation of the Indian social milieu in which the menacing powers of heredity and the demands of social custom overweigh other considerations. The communal psychology is traced out with expertness by fusing myth and realism; Anand's alembic of power is revealed, particularly, in affecting the transmutation of the whole perspectives of the old myth into the contemporary tale of a woman struggling to extricate herself from the social perversities, which are brought out with a remarkable *finess*. He is also able to transform the myth to meet the contingencies of the contemporary reality, while retaining the traditional aura. As Balarama Gupta points out :

> ...*The Old Woman and the Cow*...is the sole novel dealing with woman and her status in society. It reveals Anand's emphatic pleas for the amelioration of women.... Anand vividly portrays the wretched position of Indian woman in rural society and suggests the changes that are coming about by giving a lively description of heroine's enlightened reaction to traditions and customs, corrupted through man's selfishness, ignorance and vested interests.[17]

In *The Old Woman and the Cow*, Anand has set an ambitious project of adopting the mythic resonance of the *Ramayana*; but he has obviously failed to sustain the mythic tempo. In the *Ramayana*, the protagonist, Rama, is endowed with the qualities of both the head and the heart and he is hero in the true sense of the term; but Panchi, Anand's proletarian hero in the present novel appears to be a pale shadow. He has neither the individuality nor the moral fortissimo to defy the ossified religious sanctions. He discards his wife only because he cannot keep her with him, especially in the teeth of opposition from both within and without. His attempts to put Gauri in the 'fire ordeal' is seemingly trivial in the context of a changed situation. On the other hand, Gauri retains her essential selfhood and never succumbs to the attempted molestation by Dr. Batra. Even when she is sold to Seth Jairam Das, she does not protest, as it was customary in those that a woman once sold as a page, cannot resist the elders. But Gauri is not presented as a meek and docile woman, as most of the heroines of Tagore are. She shows her real vim in the circumstances when they become seemingly uncongenial. She stands before the village elders and boldly resists the social sanctions and their rigidities and even spurns them all, at the end of the novel. She prefers to live in self-isolation and anonymity rather than meekly submitting to the senseless social customs. For her, marriage is a social convenience, a taboo that she comes to know of it only at the fag end of her life.

Anand could have approximated the story-lines with they story of the *Ramayana*; but this would have put him into some insurmountable difficulties, for the fire-ordeal can never be accepted by any woman who deems herself to be a libertine. Gauri rightly does it so, though it may seem repugnant to a few. The tempo of the *Ramayana* myth cannot be sustained, however much the artist tries to keep it up. The story of *Ramayana* itself is full of contradictions and Anand rightly denounces the myth as spurious, though he does not catechise its moral timbre. His meaningful essay "The Old Myth and the New Recital Form" further amplifies the true purport of the novel. K.N. Sinha observes :

> *The Old Woman and the Cow* creates the legend of a heroic peasant woman in a small-minded village. It has a definite epic strain to it. The closeness of Nekrassov's poem does not in any way diminish the richness and beauty of its original conception, based on the Sita myth which is woven like a central jewel into the whole design. The novel suggests continuous parallels and links between the primitive past and the desolate present and thereby presents the most absorbing image of the human condition.[18]

The Road, published in 1961 is a variation on the theme of *Untouchable*, where the caste-element is blown out of proportion. There is neither the stylistic maturity and *finesse* of the earlier novel nor the thematic *gravitas*. As Anand himself admits : 'It is artistically a slight production' he seems to discard the high road of romance to take to the devious modes of allegory and symbolism. The story is concerned with the young outcaste, Bhikhu, who takes upon himself the task of laying the road between Goverdhan and the city to facilitate the easy transport of milk. But the construction is opposed by the caste-Hindus for the simple reason that the road is laid by the untouchables and cannot be used by the caste-Hindus. The antagonism between the two groups, one represented by Lambardar Dhooli Singh, who aligns himself with the untouchables, and the other led by Sarpanch Thakur Singh, who throws his weight with the caste-Hindus, takes in a strident communal affair. The feud assumes an ugly proportion, resulting in the obstruction of construction. Thakur Singh's son, Sanju, alongwith Dhooli Singh's son Lachman, burn down the huts of the untouchables who seek refuge in the Lambardar's house. Emotions well up and the communal frenzy is let loose resulting in communal recriminations, orgy and destruction. There is a perceptible change in the emotional attitudes of both Lachman and Sanju, when the latter takes up the construction work, and the former rejoins his father's crusade against the untouchables. A rapprochement is reached between the two families and everything ends up as one expects of literary whodunit. Meanwhile the construction of the road is over, but Bhiku walks out of the village "...towards, Gurgaon, which was the way to Delhi, town capital of Hindustan, where no one knows who he was and where there would be no caste or outcaste...."[19]

Anand has reported to have said that the novel is based on the actual incident :

> Well, it was a kind of shock to me when I went to live in Haryana, twenty miles from Delhi, in human empire of Jawaharlal Nehru, to find that the outcaste not only in South India, but in the mixed North were still consigned to limbo of oblivion. There was something tragi-comic to me in the fact that the caste-Hindus would not touch the stones quarried by the untouchables to make the road, because the stones had been touched by the untouchables. I mentioned this to great Nehru. He did not believe me. He was quite angry at my mentioning of this ackward fact. I said I would prove it to him by showing it in the 'enchanted mirror'.[20]

The epigraph from Rabindranath Tagore serves as symbolic superstructure of the novel :

> He will pass by the road
> And I wait for him :

> Many thorns prick his feet.
> He is covered with dust
> I die of shame
> Morn and Eve.

Anand considers that the road to freedom is larded with difficulties and the untouchables will have to undergo several ordeals before they get accommodated in the mainstream of Indian social life. However, the novel fails to integrate the irresistible poetic realism and social propaganda. Bhikhu is not conceived as powerfully as Bakha, who carries with him the whole 'burden of the race'. While Bakha progresses in his self-awareness and becomes initiated into Gandhian conformism, Bhikhu seems to shun all the high-ways of democratic liberalism and takes to the road in an obvious endeavour to find solidity and permanence elsewhere. This is purely a defeatist attitude which smothers the very artistic *raisen d'etre*. Though the plot is slight and the characterisation weak, it is nevertheless a brilliant piece of imagistic exercise. As Jack Lindsay observes :

> There is no intellectual imposition of symbols on the material...instead we have a natural dynamic relation between the actual situation and its total meaning. All canalized in the image of *The Road*.[21]

The Road is one of Anand's most applauded works. Though it is slender and its perspectives do not skip beyond the specific context of time and space, its overall structure depends on the superb articulation of its theme which centres around the caste-system, which has already been dealt with by Anand in his earlier novel *Untouchable;* but in the present novel, the symbolic-superstructure seems to veer round a single incident, that of laying of the road, which assumes the piquancy of interest. The Road could be construed as the road between the two groups, 'the haves' and 'have-nots'; it could also be the road between finiteness and infiniteness. The protagonist also becomes the scapegoat (as in the typical India myth) of caste recriminations, and undergoes the purgatorial cleansing through unsuspected ordeals and psychological pulls, as a mythic hero. Bhikhu, who is an extended version of Bakha in *Untouchable*, is a Herculean figure who goes on and in his task of laying the road without caring for the eventualities, and the very nearly succeeds in achieving his cherished goal, but becomes embroiled in caste-feuds, and gets defeated by the forces of orthodoxy, which still have a hold on the sensibilities of the Indian masses. Unable to resist the temptation of going away with his plans, he is caught implacably in the emotional and psychological throes. Bhikhu leaves for Delhi, the promised land, where caste recriminations are obliterated and where humanity lives in amity and friendliness. It appears that the road to freedom and salvation, for Bhikhu, is larded with hazards which he fails to circumvent and where he comes to know of the futility of all endeavours and he leaves up the task to the future generation. Though defeated, Bhikhu is never vanquished, and his taking the road to Delhi should not be interpreted as unseemly defeatism. It is the genuine angst of an existential hero who spurns everything and seeks penance in self-isolation. Bhikhu is a rebel in his own way and he could be the Camus-hero, given the right positioning. Anand simply fails to tap the symbolic potential out of the interaction of the character and situation, though the novel has a fascinating story to tell. As Mulk Raj Anand himself observes :

> Riemenschneider, who I think has been sensitive to the inner curves of some of my characters, thinks that *The Road* is a failure. I don't think he has noticed the new elements of the labyrinthine interiors, which I try to touch in this book. This novel was, therefore, not a repetition of *Untouchable,* but an attempt at a break-through at various layers of awareness.[22]

Thus, in most of Anand's novels, there is no choice for the individuals; they simply play out the roles imposed upon them by the restrictive imperatives of the society. The world they inhabit is pitiless and the heroes of Anand, more often than not, grope in darkness, unable to find promised light.

Similarly, in his short novel *Death of a Hero*, which is verily a requiem for Maqbool Sherwani, Anand fails to re-mysticise the contemporary tale of a hero who sacrifices his life for a righteous cause. No doubt, Anand succeeds in projecting the authentic picture of a resurgent India and the sacrifices of the hero, Maqbool Sherwani, whose nationalism is unquestionable and legendary. The novel deals with the post-Independence period, when Indians and

Pakistanis vied for the possession of Kashmir, now merged into the Indian Union. The brave Kashmiri people defended the territory with unflinching loyalty and redoubtable patriotism. Maqbool, the Kashmiri hero, becomes the eye and the voice of his people, though he is done to death by the unsuspected turn of events.

In *Death of a Hero*, Anand seems to have recalled from the hinterland of his memory the story of Maqbool, who sacrifices his life for the sake of his country. The character, placed in a peculiar circumstance, seems to slip out of the hands of the novelist. There is neither a perfect interaction between the character and the incident nor the development of a vision so as to be all-encompassing. The incidents are merely contrived and the background of the post-Partition days does not enliven neither the character nor the perspectives of the novel. The incident in which Maqbool is caught by the enemies and the way in which he loses his life are not fictionally authenticated. The whole story centres round the scuffles and ambushes, and ends up in the tragic death of Maqbool who becomes a martyr as well as a savior by conscious choice. Anand could have evoked the atmosphere properly and developed the storylines by infusing into it poetic realism, which is the hallmark of fiction. As it is, the characters remain sketchy and the incidents poor without proper organismic development. One may compare it with the novel by Khushwant Singh, *Train to Pakistan,* which appropriates for itself the epic immensity. It is because the novelist tries to authenticate its story adds symbolic density to his vision, never resorting to recall the incidents from the repertoire of memory. Anand's novel seems to have received a partial treatment and that explains why it simply fails to click in spite of its deft manipulation of the incidents. Even the ending seems to be a more contrivance than an artistic necessity. In his letter to his sister, Maqbool writes :

> ...this is my philosophy of life — that I love people!... I would have been more contended in facing the future, if there had been growing up, in our household, an heir to my poet's longing and aspiration. If life continues, then death, even sudden death, is as reasonable as birth, of life itself....

> ...And when you are married and have a child, I want you to remember this and let your offspring bear my name. I think your husband will permit this because I am sure you will choose an enlightened man to be your companion in life.... And your child will grow up and work for our lovely land, and through him or her, my spirit will be working for the new life in our country.[23]

He leaves the task, which he has not fulfilled, to the future generation which he thinks would take it up and sees to it that a millennium of happiness is promised forth. The novel acquires the semblance of "an epic of modern India", but only lacks the immensity and the real intensity of an epic. It is more in the nature of an individual tragedy, located in the context of the specific time and space.

Anand apparently fails to depict the conflict in the consciousness of his hero, credibly and authentically. The story-lines are developed quite unconvincingly and the characters remain card-board figures without the strength-giving sustenance. As M.K. Naik rightly observes :

> This document is far from adding anything artistically significant to action or character appears to be an excrescence.[24]

Prof. Naik is here referring to the letter which Maqbool keeps in his pocket before he is shot dead. In his letter to his sister Noor, Maqbool writes :

> And conscience...is a great force, and is the real source of poetry. For, from the obedience to one's conscience, to pity, is but a small step. And pity is poetry and poetry is pity. In our beloved Kashmir today, no one can be human without listening to his conscience, and to the orchestra of feelings without voices which is our landscape. And everyone who listens is being true to our heritage of struggle.[25]

Anand seems to have contrived the situation, without integrating it into the christological myth, which the novel purportedly deals with. Maqbool is another of Anand's proletarian messiah who dies on the cross; but the moral premises are not demarcated properly and the incidents are not absorbed into the narrative continuum. This short novel's meaning, which is quintessentially Gandhian, is best summed up in the simple statement from *The Road* : "Against the frenzy of wrong, there must be no hatred." Both are the episodes of the heart, which deal with the inherent refinement of the protagonists while maintaining their mythic immensity, not losing sight of the contemporary meaning. As Alastair Niven points out :

> Anand is tracing an almost Manichean spirit between God and Man, in which Man strives to surmount the tremendous barrier that God places in this way. The miseries of Man are victories over God.[26]

Riemenschneider feels that Anand's *Death of a Hero* is the 'most satisfying artistic achievement'. He observes :

> The novel ends with the letter Maqbool had written to his sister. And now Anand succeeds in expressing what he means by his idea of man. There is break between life and death by the main character the message he has to communicate.[27]

Anand's next novel, *Lament on the Death of Master of Arts* which was published in 1937, is a dirge, with a fictional veneer. It did not win for him any favourable critical response, for the novel is sleight in treatment and even the perspectives which it deals with, seem to have not been fully developed. Though Anand has something to say about the defective education system which merely confers degrees on the individuals, but seldom it sees to it that the individuals are assured of a gainful employment. As the protagonist cries out in a seemingly dejected mood :

> Why did they drag me into the dust by making me Master of Arts?[28]

Anand has a point, here, to emphasise but the *cri de cour* of the hero is lost in the whiff of meaningless confabulations and contemplations. Nur, after securing the Master's degree, simply fails to master his own life. He becomes incapacitated to do anything viable because he has been constantly ailing. This ailment could be interpreted symbolically as the ailment which has taken the entire generation of men like him. Nur's consumption is symptomatic of the sham and detritous of the entire Indian society which seems to have lost its rapport with the changing influx of ideas, and the societal needs. Anand suggests quite a few remedies; he wants that the entire education set-up to be re-orientated.

Anand makes his frontal assault on the inadequacies of the Indian education system which breeds discontent. As he observes :

> What is there in education, brother!
> Waste of time.[29]

He bemoans that the faulty educational system alone is responsible for the large-scale unemployment, which throws quite a few into despondency. Individuals like Nur, in spite of high academic achievements, become the victim of the erratic system of education, which never tries to bring out the latent potential in the individuals, but throws them larboard into the stream of unemployed reserve army. Though the novel was written in 1937, well before the dawn of Independence, Anand perceives loopholes in the educational system, which is purely based on the British model. The strict regimen which it maintains, and its lack of proper correlation with the needs of Indian society, perhaps has lent much supportive philip to Anand's denouement. The same is true even now, after the elapse of about 50 years of the publication of the novel. The deteriorating standards, and the vast pool of the educated unemployed are as much a concern to the Government as they are to the cognoscente. Nur is a young 'Master of Arts", a tubercular, who is on the death-bed. He looks at his life with a mixed feelings of awe and compassion, and knows that he is drawing near the inscrutable end. He very much wants to look forward to a radiant future, but there is nothing to look forward. Unable to cope with the life of misery and desperation, Nur is trapped in the life-in-death predicament, very much like Anand's earlier protagonists. His marriage further adds to his desperation and the breakdown of his health; he contacts the dreadful disease of consumption to which he ultimately succumbs. This is the most gory story of an individual who becomes the victim of environmental fate in spite of his strong desire to live. Nonetheless, *Lament on the Death of a Master of Arts* is a novel with a serious import. The action is complete within a single day and covers the events from early dawn to afternoon. Anand describes the end of his protagonist : "The body of Death lingered on the sick bed."[30] One gets the impression that the novel is intended to be a blistering commentary on the society and on the education system which leaves the individual sapped of his energies.

Anand writes : 'From the first day of birth his (Nur's) life had been pain-marred.'[31] Not only abject poverty but also the faulty education system in our country are responsible for his undoing. A degree is no passport for earning a job and in fact the erratic education system, with its quantum-based statistics, is held primarily responsible for the incalculable harm done to millions of people like Nur. It is not merely a tragedy of an individual but a collective tragedy as well, and thus pose a volley of questions concerning the global phenomenon of unemployment which has raised its ugly head in the post-Independence India. As Anand observes elsewhere :

> The whole world is in search of happiness, all mankind seeks the privileges of glory and power and wealth. But it is vulgar and stupid, the way in which society distributes her favours. The bitch has no morals. She yields herself to the embraces of any robber, brigand or cheating idiot who has secured for himself the traditional right to a vested interest.[32]

Thus, the novel is not entirely free from pontification, though Anand hopes that the gap between 'the haves and the have-nots' would be narrowed down in course of time such that equity and social justice are ensured for all. Summing up the novel, K.N. Sinha observes :

> *Lament on the Death of a Master of Arts* is a powerful, lyrical novel which surpasses all the novels of Anand in its deep and authentic search for illumination. Its lyricism is withal subtly modulated and exquisitely controlled.... The

> novelist's control over experience is indeed superb. The medium yields to the pressure of feeling at every point of the narrative. At the same time, an intellectual effort of a high order has gone into the novel's artistry, the design, texture, character and atmosphere taking on the resplendent quality of true and inimitable vision.[33]

Anand's stories are all conceived in the best of Western tradition of fiction writing, with all their density and compactness, leading to denouement. Anand transists from 'committed writer' to a 'myth-maker', engaged in the purposive act of integrating the disparate elements, such as symbolism and allegory into the vitals of his fiction. In the four novels just discussed above, Anand focusses on the specific situation — the heroine's undergoing of the agonies of domestic disharmony in the case of Gauri, and her ultimate emergence from 'home' into 'world'; in the second, the hero's taking to the road which is a road to freedom; and in the third, the poet-patriot's achieving of martyrdom, and in the fourth, the protagonist's death-in-life predicament, 'to be free to live and suffer! All these novels have a strong moral fibre and are conceived in the best of Anand's ideals and his humanist sympathies. While Gauri absolves herself of all social stigmas by boldly stepping out into the unknown destination, in the other case, Bhikhu and Maqbool sacrifice their self-interest to collective good. In the other two stories, the protagonists are neither 'vanquished nor defeated', but rather freed from the ossification of their instincts and impulses by the corroding social values which force them to prefer death to life.

Though Anand's social and personal concerns, in his short novels achieve fine fusion, myth is never Anand's *forte*. His earlier concerns with the patterns of poetic realism and naturalistic determinism coupled with his humanistic zeal for the amelioration of the lot of the 'have-nots' have given a definitive resonance and meaning to his fictional corpus. But his attempts at mythical mode, as it is adopted to the contingencies of the contemporary ethos, have not yielded rich dividends. He no doubt exhibits a remarkable maturity in form and style in grafting the old myths to the contemporary setting, but they have not by any means left any significant dent. Artistically explored against the background of his personal reminiscences, these novels simply fail to absorb the mythic resonance and merely remains as frail and weak-spined symbolist exercises. Whereas Narayan and Raja Rao eminently succeed in adopting the old myth to the new recital form, Anand's proletarian bias acts as a deterrent in achieving a fine fusion of myth and reality in the contemporary idiom of expression.

NOTES

1. Mulk Raj Anand, *The Old Woman and the Cow*, Kutub-Popular, Bombay (1960), p. 130.
2. *Ibid.*, p. 283.
3. *Ibid.*, p. 5.
4. *Ibid.*, p. 10
5. *Ibid.*, p. 238.
6. R.K. Kaushik, *Red, Brown and Gray Ideological Commitment in Mulk Raj Anand's Novel;* Ed. K.K. Sharma, *Indo-English Literature*, Vimal Prakashan, Gaziabad (1977), p. 109.
7. Mulk Raj Anand, *The Old Woman and the Cow*, Kutub-Popular, Bombay (1960), p. 240.
8. *Ibid.*, pp. 241-42.
9. *Ibid.*, p. 243.
10. *Ibid.*, p. 243.
11. *Ibid.*, p. 247.
12. *Ibid.*, p. 257.
13. Mulk Raj Anand, *Crossroads in Life,* Debonair, 5, No. 4 (April, 1976), p. 34.
14. Premila, P.S., *Major Themes in the Novels of Mulk Raj Anand*, Perspectives on Indian Fiction in English, Ed. M.K. Naik, Abhinav Pub., New Delhi (1985), p. 8.
15. Mulk Raj Anand, *The Old Woman and the Cow*, Kutub-Popular, Bombay (1960), p. 102.
16. S.C. Harrex, *The Fire and Offering,* Vol. I, Writers Workshop, Calcutta (1975), p. 137.
17. G.B.S. Gupta, *Mulk Raj Anand*, Prakash Book Depot, Bareilly (1975), pp. 95-96.
18. K.N. Sinha, *Mulk Raj Anand*, Twayne Pub., Inc. New York (1972), p. 73.
19. Mulk Raj Anand, *The Old Woman and the Cow*, Kutub-Popular, Bombay (1960).
20. Mulk Raj Anand, *Author to Critic,* Writers Workshop, Calcutta (1976), p. 124.

21. Jack Lindsay, *The Elephant and the Lotus*, Kutub-Popular, Bombay (1967), p. 18.
22. Mulk Raj Anand, *Author to Critic,* Writers Workshop, Calcutta (1976), p. 125.
23. Mulk Raj Anand, *The Death of a Hero,* Kutub-Popular, Bombay (1963), p. 92.
24. M.K. Naik, *Mulk Raj Anand*, Arnold-Heinemann, New Delhi (1973), p. 109.
25. Mulk Raj Anand, *The Death of a Hero,* Kutub-Popular, Bombay (1963), p. 92.
26. Alastair Niven, *The Yoke of Pity*, Arnold-Heinemann, New Delhi (1976), p. 118.
27. D. Riemenschneider, *An Ideal of Man in Anand's Novels,* Kutub-Popular, Bombay (1963), p. 18.
28. Mulk Raj Anand, *Lament on the Death of a Master of Arts,* Naya Sansar, Lucknow (1939), p. 12.
29. *Ibid*., p. 14.
30. *Ibid*., p. 8.
31. *Ibid*., p. 13.
32. *Ibid*., p. 62.
33. K.N. Sinha, *Mulk Raj Anand*, Twayne Pub., Inc. New York (1972), p. 45.

6

Fictionalised Autobiographies

Anand's evolution as a novelist, in the humanist tradition, could be traced back to his fictionalised autobiographies, which are curiously written in the later stage of his career though the spadework had already been prepared earlier. At the behest of Irene, Anand is reported to have said, poured out all his effusions in the form of an autobiography which ran into a copious 2000-page confessional. He wanted to find a publisher, but the 2000 and odd pages of personal reminiscences remained unpublished, though much of the material had already made its way compulsively into many of his powerful novels. In turning semi-autobiography into fiction, Anand is 'knotted' in a peculiar predicament of retaining his artistic integrity without compromising his avowed humanist preoccupations. As he observes elsewhere :

> At a decisive point in my life, my friend Bonamy Dobree could tell me (when I asked him what is the novel and could I make one out of my confessional) that anything can make a novel, provided the imagination is brought into play. This looseness of definition struck to me and found further confirmation from the friendship of Henry Miller and Larance Durrell. Of course, we were different writers with different backgrounds, but we all moulded out techniques to say the truth about our various background.... I did so without any proletarian intent.[1]

Thus the confessional mould is prompted by the artistic necessity and a desire to reach out towards understanding of Man and the universe in terms of his own life experiences. Anand's projected series of seven autobiographical novels are the products of a life-time of creativity and embody some of his ideas on life, Man and his environment. What Anand tries to convey *inter alia* his confessionals is the 'wisdom of the heart', the core of India's cultural ethos, the tantrums and the temperament of his own generation. Instead of merely updating his life experience, Anand seeks to forge a new metaphor for life, based on the 'Seven Ages of Man', a symbolic cue which he takes from Shakespeare's play, *As You Like It*. We not only get the glimpses of Anand's personal life but also the panoramic vision of India, struggling to become independent. India's struggle for freedom and the historical vicissitudes and the social and economic traumas it had undergone are all traced out in intimate fictional terms. While transforming the details of straight-autobiography into fiction, Anand is conscious of the fact that he is impaled on the two horns of a dilemma. As he observes :

> An autobiography is too personal a thing idiosyncractic of one eccentric individual. I think the life of any one of us may have some meaning in terms of other lives as well. And especially for India, where the novel...is a new form, it was important to try to and slightly impersonalize the character, so that I could look at him as character, with a certain vigilance, which could prevent self-adulation and self-pity and all the things which happen to writers of autobiographies. And I feel that the first person singular form is important because in that the felt-experience comes in with more immediacy than in the third person singular.[2]

Anand is conscious of the fact that he is writing confessional novels in the same vein as James Joyce's in his confessional *A Portrait of the Artist As a Young Man*. Anand seems to have altered his opinion in time and attempted to incorporate as much as possible from his felt-experiences without properly pruning them; he is rather endeavouring to shove the details into the service of fictional art, in gearing them up for a meaningful critical self-scrutiny. Obviously he is in search of 'human minimums' a fulcrum amidst perceptual chaotisation. His debt to James Joyce is over-whelming since the content and form and even the typical *bildungsroman* he tries to evoke and crystallise are akin to Joyce's technique of simultaneous observation. As Anand observes :

> The urges for freedom on all planes are the main motive force! The context is the whole of the life, the trauma of birth, innocence, experience of evil and good...the struggle to mirror — struggle itself in books which may be more than oneself.[3]

The first novel of the projected autobiographical fiction, *Seven Summers*, dramatises his own ambivalances *via* the first impressionable seven years of his life. Krishan Chander is the protagonist of the projected series of novels and his early perceptions and impressions form the substance of the story. Krishan lives in Mian Mir Cantonment under the fond care of his father who is kind, but all the more domineering. His intimate friend is Bully, the Budmash; and Krishan's childish pranks include the stealing of maize, cactus fruits and mangoes. He is akin to Narayan's adolescent hero in *Swami and Friends*, but shorn of his ebullience and a capacity for ceaseless adventurism. His young brother Prithvi passes away; and for the first time Krishan becomes aware of the inexorability of death, which remains an incomprehensible phenomenon to him. When his elder brother Ganesh goes to live with his aunt, he is virtually left alone to fend for himself, caught as he is amidst his own chaotic dreams and imperceptible anxieties. But this aloneness is more than compensated, for it inculcates in him a sense of purpose and an awareness of the surrounding filth and malaise. And when the family moves to Nowshera, he is put in a school, which he considers a prison, with the teacher as an inscrutable jailor.

Anand makes a careful selection of the incidents and characters and packs density into the otherwise sprawling component of the narrative. The novel purportedly deals with the life of Krishan in his formative years. He is described as a sensitive boy with a curiosity to plumb into the precocious perceptions. His mother Daska is steeped in religiosity, which almost borders on 'implicit' faith, and her room is virtually stacked with a large number of idols of Gods and holy books. Her pantheon of Gods includes quite a choice selection — Krishna, Radha, Vishnu, Jesus Christ, the Buddha, Guru Nanak and Agha Khan.

Krishan detests his mother's ill-treatment of her daughter-in-law, which simply bewilders him. Fortunately enough, he finds in aunt Devaki, a compassionate soul, simple and lovable. As he graduates in his self-awareness, he comes to know of the evils of poverty and deprivation and all forms of social and religious cruelties. Krishan's friends are all from the lower stratum of life, and the miseries they are subjected to moved him into more than righteous indignation. In one of the incidents, when Ali slaps Bakha, an untouchable, Krishan comes to his rescue, foregetting the caste barriers. He is helped by another friend Clayton, a Christian, who saves him from the clutches of Ali. In another incident, when Krishan is witnessing a Kabbadi match, he is hit by Ram Charan's stones, which he hurls at him in anger. Bakha lifts him and takes him to his house as a friendly gesture; but he is abused by Krishan's parents as they feel that he is defiled by an untouchable whose presence is felt inauspicious. In many of his novels, Anand reveals his consistent sympathy for the untouchables, and tries to restore them to their lost dignity.

In the first novel of the projected autobiographical novels, *Seven Summers*, Anand dramatises his own experiences through the first seven years of life and 'presents an intense soul-searching account of his real life'. Like Andre Gide, he feels the terrible urgency to eviscerate his felt-experience in an act of unburdening of all his childhood pranks, his abysmal joys and anxieties. The excellence of the novel lies in the personal touch with which it is treated, in the selectivity of the material, and in its faithful recordation of the intensely felt-experiences. The central burden of the novel lies in the exploration of the theme of 'innocence' and 'experience'. Anand carefully recalls his childhood experiences, though one discerns a hiatus between the actual experience and its artistic transcription. The whole novel is seen through the camera-eye of a child, from the point of view of a third-person narrator. The mystery or the charm which holds the boy's experiences comes through the lines :

> Childhood, oh childhood! How easy it is for me to
> yield to the slightest happiness and the nearest

> breath of sorrow in one's childhood! And is there any joy as pure as sorrow as fleeting as that of childhood? Was it innocence of one's soul or the sheer vitality of one's body![4]

It is a veritable paean of glory to childhood, almost reminiscent of Wordsworth's *Prelude.* Anand's main intention is to reveal the basic truths of life fissured by an adolescent's imagination and, in the process, he seems to recollect the early experiences with a nostalgia that is both authentic and self-consistent. Significantly, the novel is divided in two parts — *The Road* and *The River*. The Road obviously symbolizes the ardous journey of life. Anand quotes :

> I love road, I love to walk...leading to self-illumination and discovery....[5]

To a child, who is untouched by the cruelties and lacerations of adulthood, the road seems to stretch from one end to the other end of the horizon, without any obvious impediments.

Anand observes at the beginning of the second part :

> ... like the rivers that break down old landmarks, destroy habitation, and crops and human beings in their torrential course, carving out channels to irrigate and make fruitful other tracts, hitherto barren and spreading over all the wasted lands, new alluvial all to enrich them. Such phenomena one merely records their actions and tries to understand their causes....[6]

The river is something like fleeting consciousness, the repertoire of memories with all their ingressing quality, and the child-hero seems to move along the undulating course of the river into a possible still-centre. Thus, the twin symbols serves as a fitting prolegomena for the autobiographical thrust of feeling or experience that is being explored, here, in artistic terms. A kind of animal vitality or exuberance for life constantly modulates the episodes of little joys and lacerations in the life of an adolescent hero. Anand clearly recaptures some of the events with utmost clarity, as does Marcel Proust. His love for his mother, and the warmth and affection he shares with her, are rendered passionately into fictional terms. As Anand observes :

> My mother invariably gave me hot milk that made me sick. But I was grateful enough. Especially at such moments, when I knew that she was neglecting Shiva to come to my side. I felt I should never have anybody as much I love her, for she had not slept for nights when I had been near death and had never opened her lips except to say "May I become your sacrifice". Only the child can comprehend the mother's courage and sorrow.[7]

In a similar vein, Anand describes the ineffable bliss when he visits the sparrow house. He observes :

> Soon I could hear nothing except the isolated groans and cries of animals itinerant rhythm of parrot's speech. And I suddenly felt lighter than air, I had the sensation that I was floating upward in the sky. Then the dark whirl of the evening descended upon me and closed my eyes and I felt as though the light on the spark lit into me by my father's sing-song and lifted me on high with the strange raucous music and transplanted me to a city beyond the sky.[8]

One of the important incidents in Krishan's childhood is a visit to Delhi, with his father, where he gets lost in the melee. The episode in which he witnesses the Coronation of King George is described with a sensivity or wonderment that is typical of a child. It is best stated Anand's own words :

> The Badshah and his Mem bowed to the spectator's mound. Then they paused by the dais till a large Union Jack was lifted by means of ropes and pulleys, which seemed to me miraculous, till it unfurled to thc breeze from a lofty pole, the silver sheen of naked sword glittered across the arena in a salute and massed bands of musicians sent out the waves of sonorous and deafening music.[9]

Thus, Anand dramatizes the events of his life, as does Joyce Cary in his *A House of Children*, with a particularity and piquancy which are unique. 'It is a quiet book, set in a low key but possessing rich emotional implications.'[10] The novel impresses one with a feeling of outgrowing abundance; and its ceaseless exploration of child's labyrinth and his perceptual encounters with a myriad facts of life, of people, and of landscapes, which especially fascinate one's attention. As Saros Cowasjee points out :

> *Seven Summers* remains a rare achievement the best autobiography of childhood yet written by an Indian novelist in English.[11]

Morning Face published in 1968 catapulted Anand to literary fame. If *Seven Summers* is taken as a Prologue to the projected autobiographical novels, *Morning Face* is deemed as an extension of the same theme, with the confessional promptings carried to a point of artistic contiguity. It comes round to the articulation of his felt-experiences, interspersed with the brilliant tableau of contemporary history and politics. Set against the backdrop of pre-independence days, it traces out Krishan's progression from uncertainty to self-assurance. Whereas *Seven Summers* is simply records the impressions of the hero, from the child's point of view, in *Morning Face*, Anand charts out his hero's slow but confident initiation into the mainstream of national politics, into umpteen encounters and epiphanies. Krishan now comes out of the conservative parameters of a close-knit family background and his peregrinations take him to Amritsar, which he aptly describes as 'a city of dreadful heights'. The novel further deals with the hero's adolescent infatuation with the charming Muslim girl and his captivity in Ludhiana and his resentment of what all colonialism stands for. It intimately recounts the vicarious satisfaction he has had in the protective love of his aunt Deviki and his mother, whom Krishan implicitly worshipped. The hero's quest for meaning in life and his seeking of a temporary asylum in the evanescent world of poetry and his attempts to live like mythical hero Krishan, all form various components in the narrative continuum.

In the dedicatory note, Anand warns the readers against possible identification of the first person-singular with himself :

> I am offering this novel to you (Krishan) because though I was to be your creator you took control of the book, almost from the beginning and wrote

> yourself out, almost as if you were the author. So it is really your book and I am only the catalyst of the words in which your body-soul burns and melts.[12]

He desires very much to retain the autonomy and individuality of the hero, and his self-hood, without impinging on the character the autobiographical datum of his felt-experiences. Nonetheless, it is evident that he is attempting to fictionalise his autobiography much in the manner of Raja Rao in *The Serpent and the Rope*. The 'I' in Anand's novel is neutral and the narrative is to be seen through the perspective of the hero's motivations and actions, though one feels the presence of the omniscient writer looming large in the background.

The novel is divided into three parts — 'The City of Dreadful Night', 'The Prison' and 'The Regiment'. But the symbolic superstructure has not been properly worked out as in *Seven Summers*. Nonetheless, *Morning Face* provides an authentic picture of the Punjab in the 'twenties filtered through the consciousness of a sensitive boy, torn by conflicting pulls of tradition and modernity and a certain hesitancy to step out from the conventional taboos and shibboleths. The story thus unfolds from the hero's perspective and merges into the larger theme of India's struggle for freedom. It is a unique compendium of history and biography, reminiscence and dream contemplation, interpolated with memorable stages in the historic phases of India's evolution as an independent country. The story, in the main, pertains to Krishan's childhood, as revealed in *Seven Summers,* giving us an authentic picture of the early years of the hero. The boy of *Seven Summers* gradually passes through the stage of innocence to experience and becomes increasingly aware of his environment, its social and cultural mores. As Anand's earlier fictional heroes, Krishan strikes a disjunction from the mainstream of tradition and social customs and questions their very propriety in the changed and changing contexts, with the meaningful synthetic apprehension of life and environment, which guided all Anand's earlier protagonists.

Krishan's emotional life is mainly concerned with the three important women who figure prominently in the novel. They are aunt Deviki, Shankuntala, the wife of Doctor Chuni Lal and the courtesan Mumtaz, the mistress of his brother. As Krishan grows up into adulthood, he becomes involved in love and sex, almost with the Lawrentian *ouvre.* He passionately loves Mumtaz and comes to know the real reason why his brother is dissatisfied with his ill-tempered wife, Daraupadi. Krishan becomes aware of the evils of arranged marriages through his brother's story of domestic disharmony and disintegration. His feelings for these women are of a mixed type like that of Munoo in *Coolie,* which is ambivalent and yet touchy. The transformation of Krishan from purely a Freudian rake to an inquisitive young man, and his eventual translation into politics of his time are traced out by Anand with utmost fidelity and scrupulosity, which are rare in the art of story-telling.

Krishan's compassion for the downtrodden and the lowly and his turning away from all religious sanctions and taboos, to become a revolutionary and his overriding thirst for knowledge are all revealed in foregoing passage :

> The romance of awakening to the appreciation of being an Indian now filled me with the dream that I ṣhould try and master all the learning possible and that I should. In spite of all the difficulties, stretch my thinking further and further.[13]

The part of the novel dealing with Krishan's changing attitude towards life and his slow initiation into the maelstrom of national politics which are traced out with a minuscular precision. Krishan's mind becomes a seething whirlpool of conflicting ideas and motivations and he is unable to find solutions to the problems besetting him personally, and his country, in general. As he observes :

> I was smashed up by my dreams, I was smashed up by the thoughts of freedom and goodness. I was broken bundles of mirrors.[14]

Thus, the significant events of national history make a compulsive presence in Anand's fictional autobiography alongside the autobiographical narration of the events. The massacre of Jallianwalla Bagh, the mutiny in the Dogra Regiment, and the passing of Rowlatt Act, are interpolated into the personal datum of the hero's experiences which thus becomes an interesting historical document.

Krishan's hatred for the imperialistic British Rule is interestingly the attitude of the author's too. Anand has expressed, in one of his letters.

> Imperialism destroyed the basis of the old village life and mechanically imposed a superstructure from the top. It sapped the whole foundation of the self-sufficient feudal village, but sustained another kind of feudalism in its place. It destroyed the ancient forms, but let the fastering sores of an age long decay beneath the surface without making any serious attempt to heal the sick body, except healing it with patent medicines. It broke up and changed India, but refused to renew it.[15]

It is obvious that much of the autobiographical component has gone into the making of the book. However, it is an autobiographical novel, and not a straight autobiography. Though in the dedicatory note, Anand tries to 'impersonalise' the perspectives of his theme in order to lend to his narrative a distinctive quality of a novel, he fails to objectify his experiential vision. In the result, the novel becomes amorphous in form and content. Though Anand comes out with a timely apologetic explication, one doesn't feel that the novel has overcome needless documentation, which almost borders on the non-literary. As Anand himself has observed :

> I have written an autobiographical novel and not an autobiography. And the novel, from my point of view, gives room for newness, for departure to which a novelist might want to put it. In my case, I want to study, tentatively, towards a visionary novel. I think Romain Rolland did produce in Jean Christophe such a novel in the early 20th century, and Joyce.[16]

The novel is not so much of history as it is the hero's quest for identity. As Marlene Fisher observes :

> As Krishan gradually becomes aware of the discrepancies in the world between reality and what ought to have been or what might have been,

> his feelings of distance and isolation grow and he felt like an exile from the world.[17]

Anand clearly is trying to dramatise the evolution of his hero into adulthood and his ambivalent apprehension of life through historical time. Interestingly, it is also an artist's coming to terms with life, much in the manner of the Joycean hero, Stephan Dedalus. Reviewing the novel, Paul Verghese observes :

> While most of Anand's characters come alive, the novel as a whole suffers from a gauge and amorphous quality that proceeds from an inability to visualize clearly the objective situation of the character. This is not inevitable in the absence of any definite story with a beginning, a middle and an end and of any clear characterization.[18]

On the contrary, K.N. Sinha considers the novel to be an artistic success. He is captivated by the narrative mode and the stylistic virtuosity which are the central burdens of the novel. As he observes :

> Truly, *Morning Face* is one of the richest most passionate dynamic novels of Anand, which in a way, is syncopated, epical assertion of his prowess of a novelist. The narrative tends towards a kind of poetry which breaks time and again salient metaphor, imagery, and tense powerful rhetoric. All in all, *Morning Face* is a beautiful piece of writing offering a sentient look into the author's emotional life.[19]

Anand himself makes it clear, in unequivocal terms, that he is trying to develop a 'visionary novel' much in the manner of Tagore, in which the fictional patterns emerge from the life of unheroic-hero as he moves towards the traumatic shifts in the national history. The amorphousness is a fictional artifice, which is rather deliberate, and Anand's loss of control over his material is but a natural corollary to the nature of autobiography he is trying to vindicate and authenticate. There cannot be no judicious selectivity nor can there be a 'patterned objectivity', as one expects of a semi-autobiographical novel. Anand has observed elsewhere that he is concerned with the charting out of 'an Indian Pilgrim's progress' through the Indian inferno. Obviously, he is more interested in personal history rather than re-myticising the contemporary reality, and he is endeavouring towards something of a new kind of fictional experiment, precisely as Raja Rao does, in his later novels.

In an interview to Marlene Fisher, Anand has stated the true purport of writing his autobiographical fiction. He has observed :

> Part of my purpose of doing this long novel was to show the consciousness of a rural society developing through the years into the pattern of urban civilization, not necessarily in agreement with urban civilization, but with a view to recording the cultural residum.... My long novel is really an attempt at getting to the sources of imagination of our people.[20]

In *Morning Face*, Anand recaptures not only the 'body-soul drama' of Krishan but the mood of a whole generation in the 'twenties which went through the traumas of national upheavals even while retaining the residual energies without sacrificing the cherished national ideals and goals.

Anand's third autobiographical novel, *Confession of a Lover* commutes history and autobiography, and deals with Krishan's adolescence and his endeavours to seek solutions in the seemingly nightmarish world of the changing political scenario. At the end of the novel, Krishan finds himself in self-imposed exile in London, leaving the comforts of home and affability of his Indian friends. As in a series of cinematic montage, the novel focuses its attention as Krishan's translation to intense role-playing-as a poet and as a lover. So imbued is he in his narcissistic self-absorption that Krishan finds it difficult to come out of this solipsistic circle. At the end of *Morning Face,* Krishan is a changed person; but in the present novel, there is almost a teeming alliance between his life and the environmental pulls, a steady poise and equidistance he tries to maintain all through. He takes delight in reading poetry, comes under the influence of Dr. Mohammed Iqbal, a poet-philosopher and becomes initiated into the evanescent world of poetry. Krishan's pugnacity and bellicosity are revealed at the very beginning of novel. Krishan tells his friend, Noor Mahammed :

> We must learn to rebel...the important thing is to be — become rebellion itself! Free! Free! Free! Utterly Free! ... 'Rebellion and freedom'.... Not acceptance and death.... It is only through rebellion against everything.... I want to cast out my fears. I want to embrace people— even those who are illiterate and down and degraded! ... We will become a big people! We will make a new life![21]

He is fascinated by Marxism and accepts it consciously, almost with the passion and the ardour not of a cheap Jack politician but as a man of confidence who has had a shared experience. Here is his idealistic euphoria :

> But now there is the example of Russia, there the working class under Lenin, has cut off the head of Czar and abolished the profit system. And they are building socialism. I have hopes in Nehru. He often talks of the poor....[22]

Krishan finds in Nehru his mentor and a modern messiah who symbolises the aspirations of millions of Indians who cherished the dream of winning 'so many freedoms'.

Anand dexterously weaves facts, fiction, autobiography and history and carefully charts out the protagonist's progression towards self-differentiation. The novel virtually encompasses the whole period of Krishan's undergraduate days at Khalsa College, Amritsar, and his coming under the influence of philosophy and literature, and his pilgrimage to Lahore to meet Dr. Mohammed Iqbal, whose philosophy of the 'Destination Man' has greatly influenced him in evolving and formulating his own ideas on man and the universe at large.[23]

Anand has vividly recaptured the warmth of friendship between Krishan and Dr. Iqbal in fictional terms. There is a lengthy conversation between Dr. Iqbal and Krishan, and his friend Noor Mohammed. Dr. Iqbal informs him : 'there are two kinds of poetry. Poetry in words and poetry in action. Both are part of creative life...poetry must become reality'.[24] Elaborating his views on 'Secret of the self', Dr. Iqbal further observes :

> Some of the early vedic hymns achieved intense

> consciousness. But the Hindus reject the world. I may have been influenced by my Brahmin ancestors. Scratch an Indian, whether he be a born Hindu or a converted Muslim or a Christian or a Sikh, and under his skin you will find the Vedantist. And we are probably most soulful people in the world. But Hindu religion has destroyed everything of the vedic spirit, through its closed caste system and ritual. The making of the individual is difficult. The Koran contains much wisdom about self.... In my *Israr* I have asked for the growth of man, of the individual....[25]

When Anand had been in Bombay, for a brief spell, he wrote *The Golden Breath : Studies in Five Poets of the New India* (1933), in which he had written about the poetry of Dr. Iqbal. As he observes :

> ...I ventured to surmise, secretly that it was perhaps these moments of the poetry of reality that might help me to shape me into Iqbal's individual of the 'Secret of Self', to become a hero, a man of Will and action, A god.[26]

On the advice of Dr. Iqbal, Krishan leaves for England for higher education. Dr. Iqbal helps him financially and advises him thus :

> To be sure — it need willed efforts to make the self. Also knowledge belong to the higher sphere of consciousness. And yet in Asia we have accepted defeat, despair and melancholy. We have always been conquered, Looted, Deimated.... And now we are indignant. We have forgotten joy of living.... To grow. To evolve.... You know, son, pain is often necessary... it brings awareness. We have begun to fight against foreign rule. But not against our slavery to old customs, spells and superstitions.... Well! One of your Hindu Philosophers, Aurobindo says : "Meditate", I say "Act...." If the self is living then the ocean is limitless. Go son, conquer the world.[27]

He expresses his gratitude to Dr. Iqbal, thus :

> And I felt exalted that this sage, this poet, and philosopher was giving me his advice. He seemed to me more than my father who had generated me.[28]

Krishan is entangled in love affair with Yasmin, the sister-in-law of his Muslim friend Noor, which later blossoms into a perfect Lawrentian love affair. Though Yasmin is married off to a Muslim railway-guard by arrangement, Krishan gets an opportunity to see her when she returns to Amritsar. His meeting with Yasmin is described by Anand in the most intimate terms :

> I didn't know why, but I felt as if I had today discovered oneness and manyness in my own being through direct intimate experience of the earth and water and woman. 'My Life', Yasmin had called me. We were but images of the same love, clinging to each other, through time.... But love was only confirmation of other loves.[29]

Even as Krishan has plans to elope with her, she is murdered by her husband who suspects her fidelity. Krishan virtually becomes forlorn and even contemplates suicide but the timely intervention of his father saves him. He comes back to his home-town and sets sail on a 'voyage of discovery', and decides to go to London for higher studies.

Thus the novel deals with definitive semi-autobiographical incidents which are intervowen into the fictional maverick. Anand should have pruned the details and put them to severe editorial chaffing. As it is, the narrative is packed with inessentials which render the narrative nebulous and uneven in quality. It is only interesting in parts, but wants in unity and cohesion, which are the essential components of a novel. D.H. Lawrence's novel, *Sons and Lovers*, must have been a conscious model for Anand, but whereas Lawrance succeeds in integrating his material with the psychological motivations of his characters, Anand simply fails to amalgamate the disparate elements into the narrative action. As Alastair Niven points out :

> The author could indubitably exert great editorial control over his material. In the end, however, the mass of details does not seem cluttered but integral, for it is in the basic nature of Anand's epic achievement that a whole life should pass before us.[30]

Prof. Saros Cowasjee too feels that the novel lacks the desired unity; it is rather in the nature of a rambling chronicle set against the backdrop of national politics, without proper organismic development or functional verisimilitude. The veil of novel is never pellucid as one expects, though it could be construed as a deeply moving work, and with its cloying autobiographical thrust of feeling.

In the sequential novel *The Bubble* (1984), Anand tries to show the evolution of his protagonist from yet another point of view and largely succeeds in fusing various elements of his life into the narrative continuum. Now, Krishan is a young novitiat in London, researching into philosophy. Bursting with youthful exuberance, he embarks upon a quest for the self, for love and for unfettered freedom. A chance meeting with Irene, the step daughter of a Walsh Professor Rhys, leads him into a series of significant adventures. At her request, he starts writing the story of his life and when Irene leaves for Ireland, away from her orthodox mother, to work for the Irish Liberation Movement, Krishan becomes forlorn and lonely. His conversation with Bloomsbury intellectuals like Bonamy Dobree, E.M. Forster, Bertrand Russell, Leonard Woolf, Virginia Woolf and others yielded rich dividends. In fact the novel makes a departure from the conventional novel form by taking a cue from the doyens like Goethe, Thomas Mann and Andre Gide, mingling imperceptible longings with the passionate datum of experiences as they are filtered through the highly-charged consciousness of his protagonist.

The Bubble consists of ten parts which are in the nature of cinematic montage. The novel is dedicated to the memory of Bonamy Dobree and Valentine Dobree and is prefaced with a quote lifted out from William Shakespeare :

> Seeking the bubble reputation....

Then a few lines from Gopala Reddy, the eminent Telugu poet :

> Today is a bubble
> beautiful and multi-coloured
> Floating down the river of Time....

And finally the words of Irene Rhys :

> 'Oh let's blow bubbles.'

The novel also taken a cue from Rimbaud's poem :

> The magician is one of Rimbaud's poems, says : "We live inside a bubble, as in a womb. And in this we grow. But at times we can see ourselves in it....[31]

The theme is further hinted at in the elongated conversation of the hero with Prof. Rhys who informs him :

> The new magicians think the sperm in a little spark. It grows in ovum. The bubble opens at birth and then seals the child with each perception the bubble opens and in the bubble tries to grow and move. In the transparent glass the moves are reflected. As the skin absorbs the air, so the soul grows...something like this happens all the time.[32]

The First part of the novel is entitled as *'The Exile'* (Letters to Noor). There are 13 letters purportedly written by Krishan to Noor, his college friend, during the period between 1-10-1925 to 22-10-1925. The story grows *pari passu* with the growth of the hero in self-education. Anand uses the epistolary technique in the first part, which is full of nostalgia and reminiscence and deals with the hero's receiving of 'culture shock' in London. Then follows the diary entries documenting Krishan's experiences :

> There is an old folk tale of a woman. One night it seems, people heard wailing from a cottage and the cry; 'I am burning! I am burning! I am on fire...!' The neighbours broke open the door and rushed in with buckets of water. They found no fire. Only an old woman burbling. 'I am burning' as though in dream. 'Where is the fire?' The neighbours asked 'Inside me', the old woman said.[33]

Leaves from Krishan's diary between 12-11-1925 to 26-12-1925 form an interesting episode. It is Krishan's North-Wales Diary, giving the details of *The Ascent of Mount Snowdown.* Anand quotes from G.B. Shaw :

> Everyone is ill at ease until he has found his natural place.[34]

As he tells :

> The urgent secret desire to write a novel of the quest, like *A Portrait of the Artist as a Young Man* by James Joyce, though not an abstract to reconstruct my being, by recalling the concrete experience through which I occasionally become aware of myself in the past.[35]

Here Krishan meets Irene Rhys, who plays an important role in his life and their love episode is the most fascinating part of novel.

The title of the Third part of the novel is *Babes in the Wood* which is prefaced by a couplet from the poem by a famous Persian poet, Jalal-uddin Rumi :

> There is a beloved hidden in your heart
> Let me show her to you if you have eyes.[36]

Anand intimately recalls the details of Krishan's love affair with Irene and also his long deliberations with Prof. Rhys on abstruse philosophical realms.

Again in the part Four of the novel, Anand has used the epistolary form, the letters written during the period from 1-7-1926 to 14-7-1926, providing for the narrative continuum. Entitled *Thieves of Fire*, it gives the details of his journey to Paris and back again quotidian life in London. Anand quotes Andre Gide :

> Everything new should find us completely footloose.[37]

It is Krishan's pleasure-trip to Paris, alongwith Irene, which bears a remarkable semblance with Anand's own experiences. He writes in his dairy :

> Only my wish was to get there quicker, fly a little higher, because of Iqbal's falcon I have inherited....
> We had some superhuman superman like Gandhi,

> Tagore, Iqbal, who had rejected the money world and want new utopias, built by the weakest men through sheer courage of defiance of the prevailing anguish.[38]

During the protracted stay in Paris, Anand comes under the influence of Marxian ideology, which he consciously accepts as his *principia ethica*. He feels the necessity of a global 'revolution' of the sort in India and desires to go to Soviet Russia, the promised land of his dreams and aspirations. In his conservation with Irene, he observes :

> With my admiration for the breakthrough of the legendary Lenin I have wished I could go to Russia to see what the Revolution had done. This talk awakened my desire to go there....[39]

In the words of Tristan Tzara, one of his associates, he finds a solution for all social evils afflicting Indian masses. He says, 'After people reclaim freedom from slavery.... And they want to go back to old human condition'. He looks at Tzara almost worshipfully, and words sound like 'a revelation'.[40] He calls Karl Marx : "Prophet Marx".... The Bolsheviks have an advantage.... They offer comradeship.... And they have changed something."[41] Anand comes back to London with Irene, after hearing the news of her father's death.

Part Fifth of the novel entitled *Conversations in Bloomsbury,* begins with a quote from E.M. Forster :

> People and books reinformed one another; intelligence joined hand with affection, speculation because passion and discussion was made profound by love.[42]

The Bubble is published in 1984 though Mulk Raj Anand has already published his conversation with Bloomsbury intellectuals like Bonamy Dobree, T.S. Eliot, Aldous Huxley, D.H. Lawrence, E.M. Forster, Virginia Woolf, Leonard Woolf, Clive Bell, Nancy Conard, Herbert Read, C.E.M. Joad, Lawrence Binyon, Arthur Walley, Eric Gill and others in a Book entitled *Coversations in Bloomsbury* in 1981. The book is dedicated to 'Saros Cowasjee, who 'instigated' this serious 'gossip...'.[43] In the introduction, Anand observes :

> Exuberant naive poet hugging Iqbal's *Secret of Self* under one arm, with the sceptic Hume's *Treatise* facing me on the reading Room Desk, I discovered James Joyce's *A Portrait of the Artist as a Young Man*, with the hero's insistence on going away to 'encounter for the millionth time the reality of expression and to forge in the smithy of my soul the uncreated conscience of my race'. And I was inspired to begin a confessional novel of my own.[44]

Anand further clarifies that the talks 'with the literary men and women of Bloomsbury, as the background of pseudo-hero's struggle against the social reality'[45] are now transformed into the vital structure of the novel. His conversation with literary figures in bookshops, pubs, cafes, restaurants, and at the parties, throw a flood of light on various aspects of art and literature. It also pin-points the cumulative effect of all these men in the shaping of his sensibility. In his *Conversations in Bloomsbury*, Anand admits :

> I emerge as an electric miscellaneous and unconventional romantic, in my concentration on human predicament, the Hamletian 'to be or not to be'.... I learn to indulge in dangerous thoughts, but I began a love affair with life which lasted till today.[46]

This part of the book reveals the influence of Iqbal, the philosopher-poet on Anand in shaping his humanist ideals. In his talk with T.S. Eliot in Schmidt's Restaurant, Charlotte Street, London, Anand observes :

> Iqbal is our teacher. In a sense he is typical poet of Asia. He wants to give strength to our wills. His whole concentration upon the individual as the catalyst of action is to renew man and society.[47]

During his stay in England, he comes under the influence of Marx's ideology and Russian Revolution in which Lenin played a pivotal role. Anand has observed :

> Lenin felt that if Russia, China and India could unite after discarding the trappings of superstitions and feudal decay and throw off the white man's rule — the whole world would change.[48]

Part Six of the novel is in the form of a diary which spans the period from September 3, 1926 to September 19, 1926 and it is entitled as *Dublin Diary* (Playboy of Western World and Dierde). It gives the details of Krishan's visit to Ireland with Irene. Here he meets Madam Maud Gonne, Lady Gregory and other Irish nationalists who were struggling for Irish Independence. It narrates Irene's involvement in Irish Freedom Movement which result in her one year's imprisonment, and Krishan's decision to return to England to complete his thesis. He returns to India and finds himself involved in the maelstrom of Indian politics, and decides to write a novel on the evils of untouchability.

Part Seven of the novel is intrinsically in the nature of a journalistic exercise, which is entitled *Journal to Irene*. Anand quotes Confucious :

> It is man that makes great truth not truth that makes man great.[49]

This journal covers the period from October 10, 1926 to October 19, 1926. In the part Eight, there is a letter from his father written from Amritsar, which Krishan quotes :

> I write this letter because the relationship between father and son is blood relationship giving the parent the right to guide and mould the young.[50]

It is fairly a lengthy letter, full of advice, more in the nature of Polonious advice to his son, and reveals the domineering personality of his father. In the part Nine, again, there is a letter dated January 30th, 1927 from a 'rebel son' Krishan to his father in response to his earlier letter. He writes :

> How can a youngman held his head high and look at the stars if he is always falling at the elder's feet.[51]

He confesses, in his letter, that the "source of love" for father "had been drying up" to congeal into near-hatred"[52] just before he left for

England for prosecuting higher studies. He frankly admits to his father that :

> And I saw the contrast of affection given to me by Dr. Iqbal, Lala Man Mohan and mother against your harshness.[53]

This letter also reveals Krishan's belligerance in not heeding to the advice of his father who wanted him to enter the services of the British Government. He observes :

> I know how disappointed you will be with me for not following your advice to compete for the Indian Civil Service.[54]

He bluntly tells his father of his intention 'to make a new beginning, to start life again...'[55] and gives his reasons for coming over to England :

> And I will be free to wonder, to seek, to adventure, to live by trial and error.... I pray that I may be liberated from the scrapheap, to become 'a force of nature, away from the small minded, frightened little men always writing to the Sarkar'.[56]

He rejects his father intermittent admonitions and wants very much to follow the advice of Dr. Iqbal.

> Are you a lover? Then be firm on the path of your friend. Till God (the cosmos) is caught in your net. Beside in the free land of the heart. Give yourself up and depart towards Truth. Trust Truth as the first step on the way of 'Self'. Relay on your creative self. Suppress all irresponsible and self fancies.[57]

This letter which is fairly lengthy, reveals not only Anand's bellicosity but also shows up his refusal of paternal authority and "an urge to overcome the danger of alienation....in search of a new way."[58]

The final part of the novel which is again in the form of letter, is addressed to Irene. He quotes :

> And in this geography of hope, the polestar, you and I will be hold together with love.[59]

Krishan writes his last letter to Irene from London before deciding to return to India. He is aware of the fact that he has "to make more choices in the new life...there will be new challenges, new situations, new difficulties...one must awaken to fresh possibilities, latent in the winter's decay the opening of buds into flowers and the promise of the coming of luscious fruit on the tree of happiness.[60] Finally he vows :

> As long as I can walk. I will move at a faster pace;
> As long as I can stand, I will struggle.[61]

The novel is fairly voluminous, encompassing letters, diary entries, journals and third-person narration. The different artifices such as his early letters to Noor, through his Dublin Diary and letters to Irene, his father, allow the hero to "see himself more or less as he is or he should be". Krishan's voyage of self-discovery takes him to different emotional vicissitudes and self-propelled traumas which form the pulp of the novel. Krishan's interminable deliberations with Prof. Hicks into abtruse philosophical thoughts and his various escapades, specially with Lucy, whom he passionately loves, all are intended to be variations on the same theme. His emotional relationship with Irene, like Rama's attitude towards Madaleine in *The Serpent and The Rope*, remains ambivalent. When Irene goes off to Ireland to participate in that country's independence struggle, it helps him in a way to renew his contacts with India. In a letter to Irene, Krishan indicates his possible involvement in the freedom struggle :

> And now each of us is a fuller being than we met.
> We are free to grow into each other and into ourselves.[62]

His virtual separation from Irene, and all his eventual heartburns, seem to have lent to Anand's imagination a kind of creative ignition which he very much needed. He recollects, almost with a touch of nostalgia, his reunion with Irene in Paris and Berlin and makes a journey into the chartered destination. In fact, *The Bubble* is a fictionalisation of Anand's felt-expriences now told with the intimacy and facticity that are rare in fiction writing.

The novel abounds in images and symbols which are merely meant as decorative flourishes, but functional emblems. There is a sharp etching of characters and incidents against the backdrop of Indian politics, and the narration constantly shuttles between Europe and London where Krishan reads avidly Andre Gide, Rimband and a host of other significant poets. The central image of *The Bubble* defines and ordinates the perspectives of the theme, that of Krishan's quest for viable identity. If the bubbles of Krishan's early self-complacency are burst in the earlier part, he later musters to gather the various 'bubbling selves' into a synthetic apprehension of life and progresses in his self-education.

Anand's fifth volume of Seven Ages of Man, which he tentatively calls *The World Too Large,* proposes to cover Krishan's life through the Second World War and the aftermath of India's freedom. One can understandably envisage a change in the novelistic technique, since Anand has developed a tendency to combine the recital form of an Indian epic with the technique of Western novel. As Anand himself has observed :

> When I use the dialogue, I do it with the echo back to the Yogavashista, which are philosophical dialogue, in Indian Literature. But I do not introduce them as 'thee' and 'thou'. I introduce them as modern conversation, which is the only way by which you can be contemporary. I think the Indians have always made this mistake. We have kept the rhythms of 'thee' and 'thou'...while the situation of man and human condition (now demands something different).

And his sixth novel, in the projected series, is entitled *A World Too Wide* and is supposed to deal with the impact of the war years, and the attendant despair and disillusionment wrought by the war. It will be episodic in structure, much in the manner of Dos Passo's novels, and is intended to cover the evils of Fascism and 'the conversation with many of the European intelligentsia and move towards an awareness of what freedom means'. It will primarily be concerned with the post-war disillusionment of many of the Indian intellectuals, and the progressive declension in the moral and spiritual values.

The final novel entitled *Last Scene*, as Anand himself says, 'is a novel of struggle where one knows that the struggle one has made in the past was really not enough, that the struggle must be on a much higher plane in all the freedoms'. It befittingly ends on a note of "time's refreshing river" and "the hope beyond despair". Anand has an abiding faith in man and in his perfectability. The post-lapserian Indian Adam can now think of regaining his lost paradise, his primal roots are the confused spectacle of life. Anand's scientific humanism and his commitment to see that his generation comes out of the centuries of human bondage are evidently projected in all these fictional autobiographies.

That the autobiographies serve as fictional form to lay bare many of the unresolved tensions and enigmas is unquestionable. It becomes more meaningful when Anand's autobiography starts asserting its own autonomy over fiction. Anand's commitment* to rational humanism, which borders on the left-wing writing, is revealed not only the fundamental dichotomies involved in man's struggle for existence but also in his aspirations for a radiant future, which seem to have been annulled by the stiffness of the social convention which admits no caveats of rational ideas. The fictionalized autobiographies skim beyond the persona, and beyond the clock-time to encompass the whole gamut of human experience. Anand is neither needlessly fatalistic nor is he intensely pessimistic; his 'Indian Tragedy' is analogous to Dos Passo's 'American Tragedy' which is intended to trace man's evolution from incompleteness to fullness. His quest for a saner view of life and his unquenchable optimism for bringing about a millennium of happiness still keep him buoyant, what with his several preoccupations. The *Last Scene* may serve as fitting finale to his semi-autobiographical explorations, especially in making them viable for a mature vision in the creation of a 'solid mandala' for India's lost generation.

---

* Anand hates to be labelled as a 'committed writer' (in his letter to Dr. M.K. Naik) and believes himself to be a humanist operating within the bounds of naturalistic determinism of a Zola, a Flabuert and a Dos Passos. He aligns himself with the contemporary regional writers like Premchand. Yashpal and looks forward to the creation of a new form novel which he calls a 'visionary novel', which is aimed at projecting the total vision of life.

NOTES

1. Mulk Raj Anand, *Taped Conversation with Marlene Fisher*, May, 1971.
2. Mulk Raj Anand, *Lines Written to Indian Air*, p. 25.
3. *Ibid.*, p. 30.
4. Mulk Raj Anand, *Seven Summer*, Orient Paperback, New Delhi (1970), p. 34.
5. *Ibid.*, p. 7.
6. *Ibid.*, p. 53.
7. *Ibid.*, p. 79.
8. *Ibid.*, p. 54.
9. *Ibid.*, p. 106.
10. K.N. Sinha, *Mulk Raj Anand,* Twayne Publication, New York (1972), p. 62.
11. Saros Cowasjee, *So Many Freedom*, Oxford University Press, New Delhi (1977), p. 175.
12. Mulk Raj Anand, *Morning Face*, Arnold-Heinemann, New Delhi (1976), p. 5.
13. *Ibid.*, p. 130.
14. *Ibid.*, p. 569.
15. Mulk Raj Anand, *Letters on India*, a series of letters to Tom Brown, London : The Labour Book Service (1942) (Limited edition).
16. Paul Verghese, *Essays in Indian Writing in English*, Somiya Pub., Bombay (1974), p. 37.
17. Marlene Fisher, *The Wisdom of the Heart,* Sterling Pub., New Delhi (1985), p. 134.
18. Paul Verghese, *Essays on Indian Writing in English,* Somiya Publication, Bombay (1974), p. 36.
19. K.N. Sinha, *Mulk Raj Anand*, Twayne Pub. Inc., New York (1972), p. 138.
20. Marlene Fisher, *The Wisdom of the Heart*, Sterling Pub., New Delhi (1986), p. 136.
21. Mulk Raj Anand, *Confession of a Lover,* Arnold-Heinemann, New Delhi (1976), pp. 27-28.
22. *Ibid.*, p. 217.
23. *Ibid.*, p. 139.
24. *Ibid.*, p. 150.
25. *Ibid.*, p. 130.
26. *Ibid.*, pp. 383-85.
27. *Ibid.*, p. 384.
28. *Ibid.*, p. 309.

29. Alastair Niven, *Yoke of Pity*, Arnold-Heinemann, New Delhi (1978), p. 43.
30. Mulk Raj Anand, *The Bubble*, Arnold-Heinemann Pub. (I) Ltd., New Delhi (1984).
31. *Ibid.*, pp. 170-71.
32. Marlene Fisher, *The Wisdom of Heart*, quoted by her taped conversation with Mulk Raj Anand dt. 6-6-1976.
33. Mulk Raj Anand, *The Bubble,* Arnold-Heinemann, New Delhi (1984), p. 65.
34. *Ibid.*, p. 78.
35. *Ibid.*, p. 155.
36. *Ibid.*, p. 319.
37. *Ibid.*, p. 364.
38. *Ibid.*, p. 382.
39. *Ibid.*, p. 383.
40. *Ibid.*, p. 385.
41. Mulk Raj Anand, *Conversation in Bloomsbury,* Arnold-Heinemann, Bombay (1981).
42. *Ibid.*, p. 4.
43. *Ibid.*, pp. 5-6.
44. *Ibid.*, p. 6.
45. *Ibid.*, p. 6.
46. *Ibid.*, p. 150.
47. Mulk Raj Anand, *The Bubble,* Arnold-Heinemann, New Delhi (1984), p. 511.
48. *Ibid.*, p. 533.
49. *Ibid.*, p. 575.
50. *Ibid.*, p. 583.
51. *Ibid.*, p. 584.
52. *Ibid.*, p. 484.
53. *Ibid.*, p. 595.
54. *Ibid.*, p. 595.
55. *Ibid.*, p. 595.
56. *Ibid.*, p. 594.
57. *Ibid.*, p. 596.
58. *Ibid.*, p. 597.
59. *Ibid.*, p. 603.
60. *Ibid.*, p. 604.
61. *Ibid.*, p. 599.
62. Mulk Raj Anand, *Taped Conversation with Marlene Fisher.*

7

Conclusion

It is difficult to judge Anand's fiction in terms of a set of preconceived notions, for his themes cover so wide a canvas and encompass so large a vision that they require comprehensive critical tools of explication and juxtaposition. Anand is the most versatile and the most complex 'fictionalist' of the contemporary Indo-English literature. Prof. William Walsh is perhaps unfair to say that 'Anand lacks the concrete sagacity and the passion for the illustrational.' He views Anand's fiction purely from a Westerner's point of view which demands of the novelist too much. Prof. Walsh judges Anand's fiction from one or the other more prominent thematic angularities than what is imperative, and bypasses to examine the Indian aesthetic tradition which has largely moulded Anand's sensibility. Anand himself has made it abundantly clear that his fiction looks forward to a 'visionary novel' based not on the Western, but on the Indian aesthetic principles. He further adds that he works under the heavy influence of the indigenous writers like Premchand, Yashpal and Tagore by supplanting the European tradition of realism as evidenced in the works of Flaubert, Zola, Balzac and Tolstoy. He nearly disaffiliates himself from R.K. Narayan, whose primary concern is with the explication of the segment of Indian life, particularly that of the South Indian; nor does he deal with the metaphysical India, as does Raja Rao. He is much more interested in dealing with the cross-section of Indian social life, with all its adherence to the fetishes of values and conventions. Making use of realism as the base, Anand has explored all the aspects of Indian social life, though his locative impulse tethers him mainly to the life in Punjab; and what makes his fiction abiding is its implication of the larger perspectives of human life and conscious deployment of the inclusive concept of 'the whole man' as against the man in general.

Anand's protagonists, a close scrutiny reveals undergo a tortuous journey in life; they are pitted against the vast and menacing proportions of sham, cruelty, cynicism and hypocrisy as impinged upon them by the Indian social mores. They stumble into a series of epiphanies and, in the process, gain self-recognition, if not total transcendence. Like Faulkner's protagonists, Anand's heroes are alienated individuals — alienated both from the society in which they live and from the contingencies of the self. The deterministic patterns of the *milieu* and the ethos of change become the 'structured patterns' of Anand's novel, while his own pre-occupation with his sociological commitments forms ineluctable thematic centrality.

Anand is fired with a missionary zeal which makes him one of the finest expositors and propagandists of our time. His historical humanism is commensurate with his ideological predilections and the social values he tries to uphold. He believes in the dictum that the novelist must go beyond the surface and touch the root reality, the boredom and ugliness, which punctuates the lives of the inarticulate Indian masses. Anand is burdened by a heavy ideological pre-occupation and like his mentor Gorky, he too believes that man has to face the implacable enemy not from within, but from without. It is this time-tested society and its rigid mores that restrict the imperatives of human freedom in Anand's fictional universe. He is of the opinion that the novelist has "to recognize the fundamental principles of human living and exercise vigilance in regard to the real enemies of freedom and socialism." This is both the matrix and thematic burden of Anand's novels.

This also accounts for the agitational content of most of Anand's novels and the 'fiery pointedness' with which they are worked out. Anand does not believe in the 'Arts for Arts sake', but rather is interested in delving deep into 'the intricate labyrinth of the unconscious mind'. Surely, Anand's left-wing leanings become much more prominent in his explorations of the human condition. His heroes are not hopeless introverts but disinherited outsiders, standing as they are on the brink of social barriers which separate them from the mainstream of the Indian social life. Thus, society assumes global destructive potency and most of Anand's fictional protagonists inveigle not so much against the inviolate fate as against the rigidities of the Indian Social custom which prevents their imperative need to exercise free will. They are neither vulnerable escapists as Narayan's heroes are, nor existential sufferers as most of Raja Rao's fictional counterparts are. They hopelessly seek identity in a society that has become insouciant and 'foreclosed', and more often than not, they suffer the ignomy and shame for none of their faults. There is neither the Promethean heat nor Icarus ambition in Anand's protagonists; his heroes struggle for self-survival, and most of the time, pain is writ large on their faces. Thus, the fictional world of Anand is peopled by helpless individuals testing their strength and mien in a world that has gone to seed and where human compassion has become desiccated. Anand often uses the novel form to crystallise all these social ideas, and his characters mostly play out the themes as destined, as in the Greek tragedy.

Anand concerns himself with the lot of the outcastes, of coolies, and of socially ill-adjusted individuals. For him, as far his contemporary novelists, 'Man is the measure of all things', and in his betterment, he sees the emergence of a 'species character'. He envisages a society in which sanity reigns supreme and the rigidities of social custom are played down. But, Anand never comes out with a systematic philosophy except for the fact that his humanism is a compunded commixture of the indigenous tradition of realism and European Hellenism. Obviously Anand is interested in Man since he believes in the liberal apophthegm that 'the proper study of mankind is man.' Anand's humanism, looks forward to a more tolerant concept of 'Destination Man'. He himself has observed elsewhere that he believes 'first and foremost in human beings, in man, in the whole man.' He freely admits that he has the tremendous social responsibility in bringing redemptive options for man and in restoring him to the previous glory and decorum of social life. His own observations on life around him have provided him with a rich store of perceptions, and enhanced his humanist sympathies in more than ample measure. If Anand's novels have proletarian bias, it is not without any logistical reasoning.

In Anand's fictional universe, the individuals are pitted against either burgeoise culture or the antiquated social order and their fighting is not so much against the society as against the environmental fate. In the earlier phase, Anand is concerned with the tyrannies of caste-system in *Untouchable*; the hero becomes the victim of pitiless, social ostracism. Bakha's struggle is not against the individuals in the particular context and time but against the whole system of class stratification which extirpates the individual autonomy. Bakha glimpses in the elite Europeans a near-salvation because he is being promised forth of an ambrosial future by Col. Hutchinson; Bakha is self-aware that his future is tied up with his community, and its social betterment needs a revolution of the kind envisaged by Gandhiji. He finds in the words of Gandhi a possible redemption, the promise of light amidst the encircling gloom. In the case of Munoo in *Coolie*, the perspectives are over-stretched. Munoo is no longer pitted against the regimentations of a caste-system but against the class which smothers his fuller development as an individual. Munoo drifts from place to place doing sundry jobs, and in the process, invites the accumulated wrath of his race, as it were. In the world of utter apathy and indifference, he only gets the encouraging solace from his fellow-sufferers like Hari. He is virtually transported from Bombay slums to the idyllic Simla, where he becomes a page to Mrs. Mainwaring. Though Munoo shows no antipathy to the Britishers, his attitude towards the Europeans remains on the whole ambivalent. He contacts the dreadful disease of tuberculosis and dies ingloriously without even glimpsing the silver line in the dark horizon of life. Similarly, Gangu in *Two Leaves and a Bud*, is burdened by the class-consciousness, as an individual and as an indentured labourer, working on the plantations in Assam. Having been put to the miseries of poverty and immitigable man-induced sufferings, he is also confronted with the formidable enemy, 'the environmental fate', what Anand prefers to call it. The proportions of revolution are now spatialised; and Anand traces out a lone man's fight against the burgeoise culture which is collectively represented by the Europeans, especially in the personality of Reggie Hunt, who is determined to outmanoeuvre the natives. While trying to save his daughter from imminent molestation, Gangu pays a heavy price by sacrificing his own life at the altar of the same exploiter whom he detested. In all these novels, which are properly termed as Anand's 'mature novels', he is pre-occupied in tracing out the internecine struggle between the exploiter and the exploited. Anand's humanistic perspectives gain in both amplitude and incisiveness because he heavily concentrates his attention on the individual's psychological development and his progression towards self-differentiation. It is significant that Anand's later heroes spurn the society they are surrounded with, and move towards a new destination and a new freedom out of social chaotisation.

In writing his trilogy, which is considered Anand's most ambitious work, he traces out the transformation of his hero, Lal Singh, from an irresponsible Sikh youth to a committed revolutionary. Lal Singh's ostracism is both religious and social, and in his very act of defying the age-old religious sanctions, he is alienated not only from the family he is born into but also from the society in which he is condemned to live as an outcaste. Lal Singh is belligerent and uncompromising from the very beginning. His flirtation with the landlord's daughter Maya, and his attempted elopement with her, permanently alienated him both from his family and the society. He is later drafted into the British Indian army, the life of which is known for its horrid regimentation, and escapes from possible incarceration only to find himself in the whirlpool of murky politics. His brief love-episode with Maya, wherein lies the redeeming feature of otherwise sordid novel, is but a passing episode in the epic drama of pain and laceration. Lal Singh finds himself neck-deep in the peasant's revolt and arrogates to himself the messianic role, which he tries to fit into, but ends up once again in jail. Anand, here, gets the better opportunity to develop Lal Singh's character, his graduation from a reckless rake into a 'noble savage'. Lalu's very endeavours to grapple with the endless cycloramas of reality and his abetment with the unsuspected mutations in life, make him a credible fictional hero. He is obviously a Marxist version of the ideal traditional Hindu leader, who works selflessly for the common well-being. He prefers the life of servitude to inaction, and when he is forced into participation in the Peasant's Revolt, he finds himself an activist seeking solutions not only for his personal enigmas but collective good as well. From alienation to rootedness and then on to purposive action — that seems to be the recurring pattern of most of Anand's novels. In a similar vein, his protagonist in the *Big Heart*, epitomises all the good qualities of head and heart. Anand's juxtaposes the economical, social values in terms of the strides made by industrialisation. The machine thus becomes the totemic symbol of both betterment and self-destruction. When Ananta becomes a displaced person, without any supportive fulcrum alongwith his community, he finds no other alternative than to halt the very process of mechanisation which has thrown them out of jobs. He turns a revolutionary in his own way, but ultimately, when he refuses to allow his own casteman from breaking the machine, which paradoxically has thrown him out of job, he is done to death at the very altar of the machine. Ananta thus allegorizes the predicament of a lone man fighting with the destructive forces of rapid industrialization and the machinations of wily men who are out to exploit the poor and the lowly.

In *Private Life of An Indian Prince*, Anand is exploring the post-independence era of decadence of the princely states. With the flair of a historical chronicler, *a la* John Masters, he presents the predicament of a Prince caught in the throes of personal and historical crises. The Prince becomes the victim of the forces from within and from without and the problems which emanate in the course of his life are essentially self-made. Victor, the hero is exposed to the worst form of venality and megalomonia. He lands himself ultimately in a lunatic asylum, unable to bear the psychic pressures. His amoral relationship with Ganga Dasi, who is paradoxically his Cleopatra and Casandra, brings about his self-destruction. When his State is merged in the Indian Union, the Prince virtually loses his sanity. Dr. Shankar who is, in the words of Henry James, 'the central consciousness' in the novel, is not only the Prince's alterego, but also the explicator and a witness to all the processes of the Prince's progressive disintegration. The Prince himself is an interesting character because he typified the author's own life and personality. Anand, like his hero, has had a shared experience of having to go through all the phases of emotional turmoil and self-crisis, when he becomes deserted by his women Yasmin, Irene and Anil de Silva. The whole novel is poured out like 'hot lava' and was virtually complete within the shortest span of a month. The novel is thus an outcome of the felt-experience which is here fictionalised; it further acquires an added dimension of significance since Anand is interested in charting out the schismatic personality of his hero and his tragic ruination. In fact, all his novels are concerned with the development of heroes through unsuspected anxieties and self-propelled traumas to sophistication and self-differentiation accompanied by an increasing psychic complexity. They are, in fact, imbued with ingratiating quality which makes them thoroughly credible and human.

In his short novels, Anand tries to graft the quest pattern to his stories; his heroes seek identity in a subtle but intricately connected phenomenon from alienation to commitment. They represent not merely themselves but a whole class, not a particular even but a conglomerate fascicule of events. Though Anand's heroes are super-sensitive, and morally culpable, they exhibit an infinite zest for life. Anand concentrates on a single character in isolation, but his commitment remains the same all through, even with a considerable passage of time. His heroes retain their sanity and essential goodness in a world that has gone berserk. In *The Old Woman and the Cow*, Anand tries to graft the Indian myth to the life-story of a woman, who becomes the victim of male chauvinism. In fact, Anand deftly shoves the old myth into the recital form, but what renders the novel flat is its failure to live up to the mythic demands. Gauri, the heroine, suffers not because of her *hubris*, but because of the utter apathy of the senseless social custom which forces her to take to the road of freedom. Similarly, in *The Death of a Hero,* Anand once again rivets his attention on to the Indian politics and deals with the post-independence era of unbridled violence and the resultant volcanic outburst of racial conflict. The backdrop of the Partition days exactly serves Anand's purpose in reconstructing the significant historical events and in flaunting out the selfless heroism and sacrifice of millions of heroes like Maqbool. Maqbool's sacrifice is blown out of proportion to symbolise the mythic ritual in which the hero becomes both the victim and the victor. Likewise *The Road* is merely an amplification of the theme of *Untouchable*, now viewed from a different angularity and incisiveness. Anand is still obsessed with the theme of untouchability which finds its compulsive expression in the short novel, which seemingly lacks the former novel's *finnese*. Bhikhu, like Bakha, is the victim-hero, who is tried and tested by the antipodal caste distinctions and recriminations. He starts constructing the road to facilitate easy transport of milk from the village to the town. But when Bhikhu realises that it is impossible to extirpate the age-old antagonism between the untouchables and the caste-Hindus, he leaves for Delhi which is symbolically the road to freedom. Though a gap of nearly twenty-five years separates both novels, the problem of untouchability still remains unsolved, and Anand's repetition of the theme carries with its an overt simplification without the vehemence of social protest. In *Lament on the Death of Master of Arts*, Anand makes an unsuccessful frontal assault on the education system which has become anachronistic. In spite of his Master's Degree, Nur remains dissatisfied, having gone from place to place in search of a job. He has to put with the grilling moments in life, and contacts tuberculosis and dies, 'unhonoured and unsung'. The novel is obviously inspired by the inspiration which is extraordinary and seems to have attracted very little critical attention. Anand seems to lay bare the whole education system of the post-independent India where the obvious gap between scholarly achievement and economic fulfilment is as wide as it was in the past few decades. But this short novel leaves no dent, though Anand claims that he has portrayed the tragic spectacle in the life of an intellectual.

Thus, the study has underlined the progression of the Anand hero from cool passivity and studied indifference to one of active participation in which self-sacrifice which almost becomes ritualistic and the martyrdom he achieve is devoutedly to be wished for. It is significant that Anand has no more messianic pretensions than to present the predicament of conglomerate humanity caught in its self-cancelling travails. His Marxist affiliations coupled with his comprehensive humanist ideals make him perforce a committed writer. By and large, Anand's commitment seems to be to Man and his integrity, and he is much more obsessed with the idea of a 'Destination Man', 'a bourgeois saint'. With the unflagging zeal of a social reformer and a realist, he affiliates himself with the work of humanist writers, both Indian and European. The central burden of his fiction is to be located in his humanist perspectives, in his intransigent rebellion against all forms of authoritarianism, whether it is of society's or of State's. He deals with the inexorable alienation of man from his environs and tries to deflate him back to his own generic self, to his essential human nature, 'the species character', as he calls it.

From a purely Hobbesian creature, 'solitary, poor, brutish and nasty', the Anand hero is impaled paradoxically on the objective reality of institutionalised life which denies him freedom of choice, and the prospect of self-survival. His protagonist, in more than ample measure, endeavours to retain his essential nature as a man, shedding off all his masks of pettiness and cynicism, and progresses towards comprehending the ramifications of the integrating principle of oneness and solidarity. In the process, he becomes the victim of his own idealistic euphoria which does not crystallise into a self-willed openness to life. He becomes 'unfree', 'degraded and enchained to self-negating social perversities' and abnormalities. Anand is, here, over-weighed both by a 'desired image', and an over-enthusiasm to bring about total revolution presaging a proletarian uptopia, 'a brave new world', where all untouchables, peasants, coolies are restored to human dignity. Nonetheless Anand seems to lose, in the process, his artistic balance and becomes a thorough-bred propagandist, much to one's chagrin. Anand is obviously is interested in the Marxian philosophical community, in endeavouring to bring about harmony between man and man, between man and his society, which are the different phases in Anand's revolutionary politics. Though they are germane to personal emancipation, Anand seems to reject the concept of individualism to collectivism and seems to imply that man should have "many freedoms", if at all he wishes to retain his status as a *homo sapien*.

In his projected semi-autobiographical fiction, Anand is much more concerned with the exploration of the self than with a desire to bring about an egalitarian social order, which has been a major obsession with him all through. The simple reason why he chooses to turn his semi-autobiography into fiction, as he himself observe elsewhere, is to permit himself the luxury of intermingling personal history with the mainstream of significant historical events. Anand has written a two thousand-page autobiographical narrative at the behest of Irene in England; but the voluminous work could not be published and Anand had to wait for a considerable time when it not only got a publisher but also afforded him an opportunity to unleash his pent-up emotional experiences in the form of a confessional. Anand has virtually ended up his literary odyssey with the last novel *Private Life of an Indian Prince*, which bears the visible imprints of artistic senelity. It is basically a flawed work, with an insistence on the 'development of a single character, lacking in the 'fiery pointedness' and iconoclastic fury which fired his imagination in the earlier phase of his writing. Hence his experiments with an altogether new form, the 'visionary novel' as he calls it, gains an added dimension of significance, especially in the context of his socialist typologies and a change for the better. Anand made his autobiography the lynchpin for embarking upon the exploration of the life of a single hero, Krishan, through the seven stages of his life. Krishan's boyhood, and his formative years, and all the churlish pranks associated with a young boy, are traced out with a remarkable nostalgia and fidelity. The autobiographical events jostle into his narrative so disconcertingly that it becomes difficult to demarcate the lines between his autobiography and fiction. Anand repeats, time and again, themes from his own life, and significant historical events are mingled, in equal measure, as they are felt to be necessary for a fuller comprehension of the psychology of the adolescent hero who seems to pass from innocent self-certitude to adult experience. Anand takes a particular interest in tracing out the evolution of his character as he faces the 'rough textured life'. As Krishan grows into maturity, he is confronted by the twin psychic pulls — the paternal authoritarianism and the collective needs of the society which demanded of him a remarkable fortissimo. In these novels, the confessional vein prompts the artistic necessity, though Anand resists the temptation of transforming the material of his own story into fiction, as does Romain Rolland, without artistically balancing them. The confessional nature of his later novels have a particularity of interest in that they chart out the details of Anand's life with a veneer of glory and splendour, though one cannot rule out the possibility of the loss of aesthetic register. In his later phase, Anand takes to revolutionary idealism with a passion that is abrasively unyielding, but self-assertive all the time. This passion for the illustrational perhaps dilutes Anand's social perspectives, though he is unerring in his topography. Anand's fictionalised autobiographies are but the extensions of his earlier themes but shorn of the vehemence of his ideological commitments. He sheds his messianic role for good and endeavours to concentrate on the development of the 'Indian Pilgrim's Progress'.

Man is the measure of all things in Anand's novels and, time and again, Anand rivets his attention on his concept of 'the desired image' and the generic principles which make up the 'Destination Man'. Like the heroes of Dos Passos and Farrell who find themselves as hapless victims in a 'fore-closed' society, in which their freedom it appropriated by the collective hysteria, Anand's heroes become mute rebels in their own way. Even amidst the congeries of unconvenial circumstances, Anand's heroes remain passive witnesses to all the social and psychological traumas heaped upon them by the soulless social custom. Nonetheless, the men and women inhabiting Anand's world have infinite compassion and a certain unbuyable integrity which mark them as thoroughly individualised characters. As a committed writer, wearing the mantle of a preacher and a hard-core humanist endeavouring to ensure succour to the millions of individuals subjected to immitigable social stresses and strains, Anand tries to delve deep into the malaise of affliction almost with the vigour of a social psychologist. He combines in him the roles of a committed writer and the ferocity of a revolutionary idealist and tries to balance his art and political aspirations as mutually inclusive 'operative principles' Anand is a committed writer by conscious choice and intention, and uses fiction for the exploration of, what he calls *la condition humaine*, with overstepping the boundaries of his fictional art. But call it either by accident or sheer inadvertence, his propagandistic purpose becomes more pronounced than concealed in his art.

Anand has resented the charge that he is a committed writer, and rightly so. He feels that he is a realist, defining 'the body-soul drama' in terms of a real drama of individuals and in their fictional enactments. This, however, does not make him absolved of the charge of commitment, but rather confirms his left-wing affiliations. A closer scrutiny of Anand's fictional corpus, reveals that Anand's commitment comes out unobtrusively by the very nature of his themes he has set on hand. A lack of control or a proper restraint over his material mars Anand's fiction, though one concedes that he remains a consummate artist in spite of these minor blemishes.

Anand's fictional world is peopled by the individuals who have no obvious choice of their own; they grope for identity in a world of pitiless cynicism, and social regimentation. The heroes undergo unsuspected shifts and mutations in life ultimately submit to the forces of orthodoxy and social regimentation in spite of themselves. This necessitates Anand to present a world devoid of light and a world ossified and denuded a human sympathy. His *saeva indignatio* is directed against the whole system of societal mores and the processes of ruthless exploitation which leave the individuals as scums of the society. As in the Wessex novels of Thomas Hardy, Thomas Wolfe and Steinbeck, his heroes belong to the 'lost generation', groping for light and a foothold in the sombre world where spiritual springs are ebbed away in time. Anand's frontal assault is not against the sky but against inhumanity which characterises the typical Indian society which does not recognise human wisdom and repose and the redemptive choices open to them. Though Narayan deals with a limited segment of human life, 'a two-inch ivory', as he calls it, his fictional universe becomes credible and self-consistent, in telescoping the teeming relationship between man and his universe. In the novels of Raja Rao, one can discern the philosophical vein prompting the narrative mode; and Raja Rao largely succeeds in peopling his universe with philosophers, eccentrics and nonbeings who undergo rapid mutations of 'Being' and 'Becoming' and lose themselves in this world only to find themselves in the other world of self-assurance and radiance.

As a writer, committed to his creed, Anand has a twin roles to play; he has to tell the story, and project the squalor and miasma and decadence, and also convey his philosophy without making his fictional art rowdy and mannered or distorted. Anand is obviously impaled on the two horns of a dilemma, and most of the time, he tries to impose upon the palimpsest of social anomalies, his passion for the millennium, though utopian it is in construct. His over-enthusiasm for the naturalistic detail, and a certain recalcitrance to prune his material, result in the amorphous quality of his later fiction.

Anand combines in him the double roles of a fiction writer and a revolutionary idealist committed to a set of social principles which lend to his work a specific purpose and notation. He is also an art critic who wrote books on *Persian Painting, The Hindu View of Art, The Bride's Book on Beauty* and a book on *Indian Curries and other Indian Dishes*. He is a multi-faceted genius and his life is underlined by a passion and a humanist commitment which go beyond his art. Now he spends his time between editing, reading and working for his magazine *Marg*, which he founded in 1948; he is an active social worker, and works unflaggingly, makes his presence felt whenever there are famines, droughts and wherever there is squalor and misery. He is said to be writing a book on *Apartheid* to raise Fund for South Africa and to which the Prime Minister has promised to contribute. At present he is also editing a series of books for children on varying subjects, from India's Free Movement to launching of Satellites, at the request of National Council for Educational Research and Training. The first book of series with a text written by Anand is called *The Historic Trial of Mahatma Gandhi.*

Anand is brought up in the tradition of thorough-bred socialists and humanists like Jawaharlal Nehru and M.N. Roy and is fed by the ideals of *ahimsa* and self-sacrifice of Mahatma Gandhi. He is a globe-trotting academic, attending seminars and symposia and is still actively engaged in completing his autobiographical novels, the first of which has already come under the Arnold-Heinemann imprint with the title *Autobiography — Pilpli Saheb** in which Anand recaptures the first glimpses of his boyhood. The

---

* Mulk Raj Anand in the Preface of *Autobiography—Pilpli Saheb* (1985) observes :

"In a confessional narrative, inspired by Iqbal's long poem *Secrets of the Self*, I made some efforts at self-examination. But a friendly, though critical psychologist, who read the early section of narrative commented : 'It is good decorative prose and well disguise the truth....

So I began to put down, a more factual narrative. This may reveal, in seven parts, my growth through the various quarters and half-egos....

All my efforts in the seven parts of this experiment in autobiography will be a straining towards the extraction of the truths about my life above the prevarications."

autobiography reveals the datum of his perceptions, his coming of age and his coming to terms with life in spite of contrarious blends and twists. But one has an uneasy suspicion that Anand is duplicating the perspectives by allowing himself to fictionalise autobiographies, and by writing 'pure' autobiography in the manner of Romain Rolland and Thomas Mann. An 'autobiography' is a more faithful recordation of an individual's life, punctuated by joys and sordid facts and a myriad more things than what fiction can easily accommodate. Anand has already transposed much of his autobiographical elements into fiction and one suspects the very intention of embarking upon an autobiography is nothing but a repetition of the 'facticities' already fictionalised. If it is for sheer exhibitionism, it is understandable, and if it is for compulsive unleashing, it is needlessly unwarranted.

Anand remains one of the most powerful fictionalists in the world, voicing forth his own revolutionary ideas and thundering the doom of things. His fiction certainly produces the much needed 'shock of self-recognition', a therapeutic function which is seldom traceable in the other contemporary novelists. He may be wielding fiction as a traditional art of proselytising, but whether he succeeds in his intentions or not, depends on the receptivity he gets from the readers. The reason why Anand has become, in the words of P. Lal, 'an extinct valcano', is not far to seek. After India's achievement of independence, the social set-up in India has changed considerably, what with governmental legislation and its commitment to better the life of the 'have-nots'. The inhumanity of man to man has been lessened to a considerable degree and the social equality has become the war-cry of the new generation. Though the caste barriers still prevail, the edges of caste cruelty and recriminations are roughed out. And in this changed and changing contexts, Anand's ideological commitments seem to have lost their relevance; and his turning away from fiction to autobiography reads much more than what the leading critics interpret.

Selected Bibliography

WORKS BY MULK RAJ ANAND

Fiction

1. *Untouchable,* Lawrence & Wishart, London, 1935.
2. *Coolie*, Lawrence & Wishart, London, 1936.
3. *Two Leaves and a Bud*, Lawrence & Wishart, London, 1937.
4. *Lament on the Death of Master of Arts,* Naya Sansar, Lucknow, 1938.
5. *The Village,* Jonathan Cape, London, 1939.
6. *Across the Black Water,* Jonathan Cape, London, 1940.
7. *The Sword and the Sickle,* Jonathan Cape, London, 1942.
8. *The Big Heart,* Hutchinson International Authors, London, 1945.
9. *Seven Summers,* Hutchinson International Authors, London.
10. *Private Life of an Indian Prince*, Hutchinson International, London, 1953.
11. *The Old Woman and the Cow,* Kutub-Popular, Bombay, 1960.
12. *The Road,* Kutub-Popular, Bombay, 1961.
13. *Death of a Hero*, Kutub-Populár, Bombay, 1963.
14. *Morning Face,* Kutub-Popular, Bombay, 1968.
15. *Confession of a Lover,* Arnold-Heinemann, New Delhi, 1976.
16. *The Bubble*, Arnold-Heinemann, New Delhi, 1984.
17. *Autobiography*-Part I, *Pilpli Saheb*, Arnold-Heinemann, New Delhi, 1981.

COLLECTIONS OF SHORT STORIES AND NON-FICTION

1. *The Lost Child and Other Stories*, Printed privately by Eric Gill, Piggotts, High Wycombe, Buck, 1934.
2. *The Barber's Trade Union and Other Stories*, Jonathan Cape, London, 1944.
3. *Indian Fairy Tales* (Retold by Mulk Raj Anand), Kutub-Popular, Bombay, 1946.
4. *The Tractor and the Corn Goddess and Other Stories,* Thacker & Company, Bombay, 1947.
5. *Reflections on the Golden Bed and Other Stories,* Current Book House, Bombay, 1954.
6. *Selected Stories,* Foreign Language Publishing House, Moscow, 1954.
7. *The Power of Darkness and Other Stories*, Jaico Publishing House, Bombay, 1959.
8. *Aesop's Fables* (Retold by Mulk Raj Anand), Dhawale Popular, Bombay, 1960.
9. *More Indian Fairy Tales* (Retold by Mulk Raj Anand), Kutub-Popular, Bombay, 1961.
10. *Lajwanti and Other Stories*, Jaico Publishing House, Bombay, 1966.
11. *Between Tears and Laughter*, Sterling Publishers, New Delhi, 1973.
12. *Folk Tales of Punjab,* Sterling Publishers, New Delhi, 1974.

Non-Fiction

13. *Persian Paintings,* Faber & Faber, London, 1930.
14. *Curries and Other Indian Dishes*, Desmond Harmsworth, London, 1932.
15. *The Hindu View of Art,* George Allen & Unwin, London, 1933.
16. *The Golden Breath,* Studies in Five Poets of the New India, John Murrey, London, 1933.
17. *Marx and Engels on India*, Socialist Book Club, Allahabad, 1939.

18. *Letters on India*, The Labour Book Service, George Routedge & Sons, London, 1942.

19. *Apology for Heroism*, Lindsay Drummond, London, 1946.

20. *Homage to Tagore*, Sangam Publishers, Lahore, 1946.

21. *The Birde's Book of Beauty* (in collaboration with Krishna Hutheesing), Kutub-Popular, Bombay, 1947.

22. *On Education*, Hind Kitabs, Bombay, 1947.

23. *The King-Emperor's English*, Hind Kitab, Bombay, 1948.

24. *The Story of India,* Kutub Popular, Bombay, 1948.

25. *Lines Written to an Indian Air*, Nalanda Publications, Bombay, 1949.

26. *The Indian Theatre*, Dennis Dobson, London, 1950.

27. *The Story of Man,* Sikh Publishing House, Amritsar, 1954.

28. *The Dancing Foot*, Ministry of Information & Broadcasting, New Delhi, 1957.

29. *The India in Colour,* McGraw-Hill, New York, 1958.

30. *Kama Kala*, Nagel Company, Geneva, New York, 1958.

31. *Homage to Khajuraho* (in collaboration with Stella Kramrisch), Marg Publications, Bombay, 1962.

32. *Is There a Contemporary Indian Civilization*? Asia Publishing House, Bombay, 1963.

33. *The Story of Chacha Nehru*, Rajpal & Sons, Bombay, 1965.

34. *The Valcano* (some comments on the Development of Rabindranath Tagore's Aesthetic Theories and Art Practice), M.S. University, Baroda, 1967.

35. *Roots and Flowers* (Karnatak University), Dharwar, 1972.

36. *Author to Critic*, The letters of Mulk Raj Anand and Saros Cowasjee, Ed. Saros Cowasjee, Writers Workshop, Calcutta, 1973.

37. *Conversation in Bloomsbury*, Arnold-Heinemann, New Delhi, 1981.

ARTICLES

1. 'Towards a New Indian Literature', *Left Review*, Vol. 2, No. 12, Sept. 1936.
2. 'Anglo-Indian Literature', *Life and Letters To-Day*, Vol. 15, No. 5, Autumn, 1936.
3. 'The Censorship in India', *Bombay Chronicle*, 27 December 1936.
4. 'Homage to Spain', *Congress Socialist*, Vol. 2, 1 May 1937, 15 May 1937, 29 May 1937, 11 September 1937.
5. "English Novels of the Twentieth Century on India", *Asiatic Review*, N.S. 39 (July, 1941), 244-51.
6. 'National Freedom in the U.S.S.R.' *Labour Monthly*, Vol. 24, November 1942.
7. "Rabindranath Tagore", *New Spirit* (Ed.) by J.W.L. Martin, London : Dennis Dobson Ltd., 1946.
8. "Introduction" to Rice and Other Stories by K.A. Abbas, Bombay International Book House, 1947.
9. "A Writer's Confession of His Faith", *Bharat Jyoti*, 27 April 1952.
10. "New Bearings in Indian Literature", *Literary Review*, India Number, Summer, 1961.
11. "Is Indian Literature Sufficiently Indian?", *United Asia*, XIII, 6 (Nov-Dec. 1961).
12. "Trends in the Novel", *Cultural Forum* (Tagore Number), 1961.
13. "The Place of a Gifted Individual in Indian Society", *The Year Book of Education*, London, 1961.
14. "The Writer's Role in National Integration : A Discussion", *Indian Literature*, V. No. 1 (1962), 50-58.
15. "A Letter", *A Souvenir Volume of Appreciations* (The Radhakrishan Number), Madras—Hyderabad, 1962.
16. "Creative Writing in the Present Crisis", *Indian Literature*, Vol. 1 (1963), 70-77.

17. "The Place of Art in University Education", *Journal of University Education*, II, 1, September 1963.

18. "The Concept of an Asian Mind", *Contemporary Indian Literature*, IV (Oct.-Nov. 1964), 6-7 and 8-9.

19. "Jawaharlal Nehru", *Cultural Forum* (Special Number on Jawaharlal Nehru), VI. 4, November 1964.

20. "How I Became a Writer", *Contemporary Indian Literature* V, 11-12 (November-December 1965), 13-15.

21. "Is Universal Criticism Possible?" *The Literary Criterion*, VII, (Winter, 1965), 68-75.

22. "Kipling and Forster", *Quest*, No. 47 (1965), 41-55.

23. "A Note on Modern Indian Fiction", *Indian Literature*, VIII, No. 1 (1965), 44-57.

24. "What Shakespeare Means to Me", *Contemporary Indian Literature*, (May-July 1965).

25. "The One and the Many : Some Changing Social Patterns of New India", *United Asia*, XVIII, 1 (January-February 1966).

26. "The Role of Creative Writers and Artists in the Developing Countries of Afro-Asia", *Afro-Asia and World Affairs*, III, No. 1 (Spring, 1966), 18-21.

27. "The Sources of Creative Writing", *Indian Literature*, VII (September 1967).

28. "Whither India?", *Gandhi Marg*, 44 XI, 4, October 1967.

29. "Speech", *Soviet Review*, V. 21 (March 26, 1968).

30. "The Question of Modernity", *Modernity and Contemporary Indian Literature, Simla : Institute of Advanced Study*, 1968, pp. 43-49.

31. "The Story of My Experiments with a White Lie", *Critical Essays on Indian Writing in English* (Ed.) M.K. Naik, S.K. Desai and G.S. Amur, Dharwar, 1968.

32. "When Our Hearts Were Young and Gay", *Times of India*, Bombay, 22nd December 1968.

33. "What Good is Literature For?', *The Banasthali Patrika*, Year 5, No. 14, January 1970.

34. 'The Spirit of Man in Indian and South-East Asian Culture Since the End of Western Domination', *Afro-Asian Writings*, Vol. 2, No. 6, October 1970.
35. 'Burning Conscience', *Afro-Asian Writings*, July 1971.
36. "Pigeon-Indian : Some Notes on Indian-English Writing", *Studies in Australian and Indian Literature* (Ed.) C.D. Narasimhaiah and S. Nagarajan (Indian Council for Cultural Relations, 1971).
37. "Anglo-Saxon Attitudes : Twentieth Century English Fiction about India", *The Image of India in Western Creative Writing* (Ed.) M.K. Naik, S.K. Desai and Kallapur, Dharwar, 1971.
38. 'Tradition and Innovation', *Lotus*, January 1972 (Formerly Afro Asian Writings).
39. "What Price Red Book, Comrade?" : Open Letter to Mao, *Blitz*, Bombay, 12 February 1972.
40. "The Vision of Bhai Vir Singh", *The Tribune*, 13 February, 1972.
41. "The Changelink — An Indo-Anglian Novelist's Credo", *Indian and Foreign Review*, Vol. 9, No. 23, 15 September 1972.
42. "Trends in the Modern Indian Novel", *Journal of Indian Writing in English*, January 1973.
43. "Macaulay's Vociferous Logic", *Indian and Foreign Review*, Vol. 10, No. 24, 1 October 1973.

SECONDARY SOURCES

I. *Works on Mulk Raj Anand*

Books on Anand

1. Berry, Margeret, *Mulk Raj Anand : The Man and the Novelist*, Amsterdam : Oriental Press, 1971.
2. Cowasjee, Saros, *So Many Freedoms,* A Study of Major Fiction of M.R. Anand, Oxford University Press, New Delhi, 1977.

3. Fisher Marlene, *The Wisdom of the Heart*, A Study of M.R. Anand, Sterling Pub., New Delhi, 1985.

4. Gupta, G.S. Balarama, *Mulk Raj Anand,* A Study of his Fiction in Human Perspective, Prakash Book Depot, Bareilly, 1974.

5. Lindsay, Jack, *The Elephant and the Lotus*, A Study of the Novels of Mulk Raj Anand, Kutub-Popular, Bombay, 1965.

6. Murthi, K.V.S., *The Sword and the Sickle* — A Study of M.R. Anand's Novels, Geeta Book House, Mysore, 1983.

7. Naik, M.K., *Mulk Raj Anand,* Anrold-Heinemann, New Delhi, 1973.

8. Niven Alastair, *Yoke of Pity,* Arnold-Heinemann, New Delhi, 1978.

9. Paul, P.S., *The Novels of Mulk Raj Anand*, A Thematic Study, Sterling Pub., New Delhi, 1983.

10. Rajan, P.K., *Studies in Mulk Raj Anand,* Abhinav Pub., New Delhi, 1986.

11. Riemenschneider, D., *An Ideal of Man in Anand's Novels,* Kutub-Popular, Bombay, 1967.

12. Sinha, K.N., *Mulk Raj Anand*, Twayne Publishers, New York, 1972.

13. Sharma, K.D. (Ed.), *Perspectives on Mulk Raj Anand,* Vimal Prakashan, Ghaziabad, 1984.

II. *Individual Chapters in Books*

1. Amur, G.S. & *et al.*, *Essays on Comparative Literature and Linguistics*, Sterling Pub., New Delhi, 1984.

2. Amur, G.S., *Indian Reading in Commonwealth Literature,* Sterling Pub., New Delhi, 1984.

3. Bald, S.R., *Novelists and Political Consciousness,* Literary Expression of Indian Nationalism 1917-1947, 1982.

4. Baker, Denys Val, Ed., *Writers Today*, Sidgwick & Jackson, London, 1948.

5. Cowasjee Saros, *Author to Critics*, The Letters of M.R.

Anand to Saros Cowasjee, Writers Workshop, Calcutta, 1973.

6. Derrett, M.E., *The Modern Indian Novel in English*, A Comparative Approach, University Libre de Bruxelles, 1966.
7. Dhawan R.K., *Modern Indo-English Fiction,* Bahri Pub., New Delhi, 1982.
8. Dhawan, R.K., *Explorations in Modern Indo-English Fiction,* Bahri Pub. (P) Ltd., New Delhi, 1982.
9. Goyal, B.S., *Culture and Commitment — Aspects of Indian Literature in English,* Salabh Book House, Meerut, 1984.
10. Henderson, Philip, *The Novel Today*, The Bodley Head, London, 1936.
11. Hemenway Stephen, *The Novel of India*, Vol. I & II, Writers Workshop, Calcutta, 1975.
12. Harrex, S.C., *The Fire & The Offering*, The English-Language Novel of India, 1935-1970, Writers Workshop, Calcutta, 1977.
13. Iyengar, K.R., Srinivasa, *Indian Writing in English,* Asia Publishing House, Bombay, 1962.
14. Iyengar, K.R.S., *Indian Literature Since Independence*, A Symposium : Sahitya Akademi, 1973.
15. Jotwani Motilal, *Contemporary Indian Literature and Society*, Heritage Publishers, New Delhi, 1979.
16. Jha Rama, *Gandhian Thought and Indo-Anglian Novelists*, Chanakya Pub., Delhi, 1983.
17. Kachru, B.B., *The Indianization of English*, Oxford University Press, Delhi, 1983.
18. Kalinnikova Elena J., *Indian English Literature : A Perspective*, Vimal Prakashan, Ghaziabad, 1982.
19. Krishna Swamy Shantha, *The Woman in Indian Fiction*, Ashish Pub. House, New Delhi, 1984.
20. Mehta, P.P., *Indo-Anglian Fiction*, An Assessment, Prakash Book Depot, Bareilly, 1968.
21. Mukherjee, Meenakshi, *The Twice Born Fiction*, Heinemann Educational Book, New Delhi, 1971.

22. Melwani Murlidas, *Themes in Indo-Anglian Literature,* Prakash Book Depot, Bareilly, 1977.

23. Mahle, H.S., *Indo-English Fiction, Some Perceptions*, Jainsons Publications, New Delhi, 1985.

24. Malik Yogendra, *Politics and the Novel in India*, Orient Longman Ltd., Bombay, 1978.

25. Mc Cuthion David, *Indian Writing in English*, Writers Workshop, Calcutta, 1973.

26. Mokashi-Punekar, S., *The Indo-Anglian Creed.*

27. Naik, M.K. *et al.* (eds.), *Critical Essays on Indian Writing in English*, Karnatak University, Dharwar, 1968.

28. Narsimhaiah, C.D., *The Wirter's Gandhi*, Punjabi University, Patiala, 1967 — *The Swan and the Eagle*, Indian Institute of Advance Study, Simla, 1969.

29. Nicholson, Kai, *A Presentation of Social Problems in the Indo-Anglian and the Anglo-Indian Novel*, Jaico Publishing House, Bombay, 1972.

30. Naik, M.K., *Dimension of Indian English Literature*, Sterling Publishing, New Delhi, 1984.

31. Naik, M.D. (Ed.), *Perspectives on Indian Fiction in English*, Abhinav Pub., New Delhi, 1985.

32. Prasad, H.M. (Ed.), *Response : Recent Revaluations of Indian Fiction in English* : Prakash Book Depot, Bareilly, 1985.

33. Press John, *Commonwealth Literature—Unity and Diversity of Culture*, 1967.

34. Rao, A.V. Krishna, *The Indo-Anglian Novel and the Changing Tradition*, Rao & Raghavan, Mysore, 1972.

35. Riemenschneider, D., *An Ideal of Man in Anand's Novels,* Kutub-Popular, Bombay, 1967.

36. Ram, Atma, *Essays on Indian English Literature*, Purimal Prakashan, Calcutta, 1984.

37. Rao, K.R., *The Fiction of Raja Rao*, Parimal Prakashan, Aurangabad, 1980.

38. Reddy, G.A., *Indian Writing in English & its Audience*, Prakash Book Depot, Bareilly, 1979.

39. Roy, M.N., *New Humanism — A Manifesto*, Ajanta Pub., Delhi, 1981.

40. Raghavacharyulu, D.V.K., *Two Fold Voice : Essay on Indian Writing in English*, Guntur : Naovidaya Pub., The Unpunctual Pen, 1971.

41. Sinha, K.D. (Ed.), *Indian Writing in English*, Heritage Publishers, New Delhi, 1979.

42. Sharma, K.K., *Indo-English Literature*, Vimal Prakashan, Gaziabad, 1962.

43. Shrirwadkar Meena, *Image of Woman in the Indo-Anglian Novel*, Sterling Pub., New Delhi, 1979.

44. Verghese, C.P., *Essays on Indian Writing in English*, N.V. Publications, New Delhi, 1975.

45. William, Walsh, *A Human Idiom* : *Literature and Humanity*, Chatto & Windus, London, 1964.

William, Walsh, *A Manifold Voice*, Chatto & Windes, London, 1964.

William Walsh, *Commonwealth Literatures,* Oxford University Press, London, 1973.

46. Williams, Haydn More, *Studies in Modern Fiction in English*, 2 Vols., Writers Workshop, Calcutta, 1973.

III. *Other Critical Articles, Reviews, Chapter in Books*

1. Abidi, S.Z.H., "Mulk Raj Anand's Coolie : A Critical Study", Bereilly : Prakash Book Depot, 1976.

2. Abidi, S.Z.H., "Mulk Raj Anand's Untouchable : A Critical Study", Bareilly, Prakash Books Depot, 1976.

3. Asnani, Shyam, M., "The Indian Princes : Their Portrayal in the Indo-English Novel," *Commonwealth Quarterly*, Vol. III, No. 11, June 1979.

4. Asnani, Shyam, M., "Form and Technique in Mulk Raj Anand's Novels", *Indian Scholar*, Vol. II, No. 2, July 1980.

5. Asnani, Shyam, M., "Socio-Political Concerns in the Novels of Dr. Mulk Raj Anand", *Triveni*, April-June 1976.

6. Asnani, Shyam, M., "The Theme of East-West Encounter in the Novels of Mulk Raj Anand", *Littcrit*, Vol. IV, No. 2, Dec. 1978.

7. Asnani, Shyam, M., "Untouchability and Mulk Raj Anand's Untouchables", *The Banasthali Patrika*, Year 6, No. 16, Jan. 1971.

8. Badal, R.K., "Indo-Anglian Literature : An Outline", Bareilly : Prakash Book Depot, 1975.

9. Bhattacharya, Bhabani, "Indo-Anglian", *The Novel in Modern India* (Ed.) Iqbal Bakhtiyar, Bombay, The P.E.N. All-India Centre, 1964.

10. Bose, Amalendu, "Indian Writing in English." *Indian Writing in English*, Ed. K.N. Sinha, Delhi, Heritage Publishers, 1979.

11. Brunton, T.D., "Indian in Fiction — The Heritage of Indianness", *Critical Essays on Indian Writing in English*, (Ed.) M.K. Naik *et al.*, Madras, The Macmillan Company of India, 1972.

12. Bald, S.R., "Politics of a Revolutionary Elite : A Study of Mulk Raj Anand's Novels", *Modern Asia Studies*, Vol. 8, No. 4, 1974.

13. *Blitz*, "Untouchables Forever!", 19 August 1972.

14. Brown, F.J., "Review of the Big Heart", *Life and Letters To-day*, Vol. 47, No. 99, November 1945.

15. Brown, F.J., "Prophet of Revolution", *Bharat Jyoti*, 15 December 1946.

16. R.K. Bhattacharya, "Two Leaves and a Bud" : Truth and Fiction, *Kakatiya Journal of English Studies*, Vol. II, No. 1, Spring 1977. "Mulk Raj Anand Special Number", Department of English, Kakatiya University, Warangal.

17. Catter, D., "Probing Identities : Untouchable, Things Fall Apart and This Earth, My Brother...", *The Literary Criterion*, Vol. XIX, No. 3, 1979.

18. Chandah, R.P., "The Mahatma in Modern Indo-English Fiction", *The Indian P.E. No.*, Vol. XXXXII, Nos. 11-12, Nov.-Dec. 1976.
19. Chandah, R.P., "The Partition in Indo-Anglian Fiction", *The Journal of Indian Writing in English*, Vol. V, No. 20, July 1977.
20. Chinneswararao, G.J., "Anand's Private Life and Malgaonkar's Princes", *The Journal of Indian Writing in English*, Vol. IV, No. 1, Jan. 1976.
21. Cowasjee Saros, "Anand's Literary Creed", *The Journal of Indian Writing in English*, Vol. I, No. 1, Jan. 1973.
22. Cowasjee Saros, "Anand's Princes and Proletarians", *The Literary Half yearly*, Vol. IX, No. 2, 1968.
23. Cowasjee Saros, "Anand's Two Leaves and a Bud", *Indian Literature*, Vol. XVI, Nos. 3 & 4, July-Dec. 1973.
24. Cowasjee Saros, "The Big Heart : A New Perspective", *ACLALS Bulletin*, Fourth Series, No. 2, 1975.
25. Cowasjee Saros, "Coolie : An Assessment", Delhi : Oxford Univ. Press, 1976.
26. Cowasjee Saros, "Mulk Raj Anand's Coolie : An Appraisal", *The Banasthali Patrika*, Year 8, No. 19, July 1972.
27. Cowasjee Saros, "Mulk Raj Anand and His Critics", *The Banasthali Patrika*, Year 4, No. 12, January 1969.
28. Cowasjee Saros, "Mulk Raj Anand : A Profile", *The Illustrated Weekly of India*, 4 May 1969.
29. Cowasjee Saros, "Mulk Raj Anand's The Sword and the Sickle", *World Literature Written in English*, Vol, XIV, No. 2, Nov. 1975.
30. Cowasjee Saros, "Mulk Raj Anand's Untouchable : An Appraisal," *Indo-English Literature : A Collection of Critical Essays* (Ed.) K.K. Sharma, Ghaziabad : Vimal Prakashan, 1977.
31. Cowasjee Saros, "Princes and Politics", *The Literary Criterion*, Vol. VIII, No. 4, Summer 1969.
32. Cowasjee Saros, "Review of Margaret Berry's Mulk Raj

Anand : The Man and the Novelist", Amsterdam : Oriental Press, 1971.

33. Cowasjee Saros, "Review of Mulk Raj Anand's Morning Face", *Indian Literature*, Vol. XIII, No. 1, 1970.

34. Clare, Tullis, "Review of The Sword and the Sickle", *Time and Tide*, Vol. 33, No. 17, 25 April 1942.

35. Collis, Maurice, "Review of Across the Black Water", *Time and Tide*, Vol. 21, No. 48, 30 November 1940.

36. Cowasjee, Saros, 'Mulk Raj Anand; Princes and Proletarians', *The Journal of Commonwealth Literature*, No. 5, July 1968.

37. Cowasjee, Saros, "Mulk Raj Anand : The Early Struggles of Novelist", *The Journal of Commonwealth Literature*, Vol. 7, No. 1, June 1972.

38. Cowasjee, Saros, "Mulk Raj Anand and the B.B.C.", *Indian and Foreign Review*, Vol. 10, No. 10, 1 March 1973.

39. Cowasjee, Saros, "Mulk Raj Anand's Confession of a Lover", *The International Fiction Review*, Vol. 14, No. 1, January 1977.

40. Curis, Anthony, "Dhal and Diaghilav", *The New Statesman and Nation*, Vol. 42, No. 170, 8 September 1951.

41. Das, Kamala, "Review of Mulk Raj Anand's Confession of a Lover", *Youth Times*, Sept. 1976.

42. Das, J.P., "Review of Saros Cowasjee, So Many Freedom", *Commonwealth Quarterly*, Vol. III, No. 10, March 1979.

43. Davies, Bryn, M., "British and Indian Images of India," *Readings in Commonwealth Literature*, Ed. William Walsh, Oxford : Clarendon Press, 1973.

44. Derrett, M.E., "The Modern Indian Novel in English, A Comparative Approach", Bruxlles : Universite Libre de Bruxlles, 1966.

45. Desai, Anita, "The Indian Writer's Problems", *ACLALS Bulletin*, Fourth Series, No. 2, 1975.

46. Dutt, Prabhat Kumar, "Mulk Raj Anand in Relation to Tagore, Prem Chand and Sarat Chatterjee", *Contemporary Indian Literature*, Vol. V. Nos. 11-12, Nov.-Dec. 1965.

47. Debjani Chatterjee, "Gandhi's Influence on Anand and his Fiction", *Kakatiya Journal of English Studies*, Vol. II, No. 1, Spring, 1977, Mulk Raj Anand Special Number, Department of English, Kakatiya University, Warangal.

48. D. Ramakrishna, "Anand's ideas of the Novel", *Kakatiya Journal of English Studies*, Vol. II, No. 1, Spring, 1977, Mulk Raj Anand Special Number, Department of English, Kakatiya University, Warangal.

49. D. Riemenschneider, "Death of a Hero", *Kakatiya Journal of English Studies*, Vol. II, No. I, Spring, 1977, Mulk Raj Anand Special Number, Department of English, Kakatiya University, Warangal.

50. Dutt, Prabhat Kumar, "English and India", Ed. M. Manual and K. Ayyappa Panikar, Madras : Macmillan India Press, 1978.

51. Dutt, Prabhat Kumar, 'Experimentation with Language in Indian Writing', (Ed.) S.K. Desai, Kolhapur : Shivaji University, 1974.

52. Dutt, Prabhat Kumar, 'Fiction and the Reading Public In India", (Ed.) C.D. Narsimhaiah, Mysore : Univ. of Mysore, 1967.

53. E. Nageswara Rao, "Dialogue in Forster and Anand : A Contrastive Analysis", *Kakatiya Journal of English Studies*, Vol. II, No. 1, Spring 1977, Mulk Raj Anand Special Number, Department of English, Kakatiya University, Warangal.

54. Edgell Rickword, "Three Views on Coolie", *Kakatiya Journal of English Studies*, Vol. II, No. 1, Spring, 1977, Mulk Raj Anand Special Number, Department of English, Kakatiya University, Warangal.

55. Edward Burra, "Three views on Coolie", *Kakatiya Journal of English Studies*, Vol. II, No. 1, Spring 1977, Mulk Raj Anand Special Number, Department of English, Kakatiya University, Warangal.

56. Fisher, Marlene, "Interview with Mulk Raj Anand : May 19,

1973 Khandala", *World Literature Written in English*, Vol. 13, No. 1, April 1974.

57. Fisher, Merlene, "Mulk Raj Anand's Confessional Novels", *The Journal of Indian Writing in English*, Vol. IV, No. 2, July 1976.

58. Fisher, Marlene, "Mulk Raj Anand : The Novelist as Novelist", *Punjab University Research Bulletin — Arts*, Vol. IV, No. 1, April 1973.

59. Fisher, Marlene, "The Shape of Lostness : Mulk Raj Anand's Short Stories", *The Journal of Indian Writing in English*, Vol. II, No. 1, January 1974.

60. Fiske, Adele, M., "Karms in South Indian Novels", *Literature East and West*, Vol. X, Nos. 1-2, 1966.

61. Godak, V.K., "English in India : Its Present and Future", Bombay : Asia Publishing House, 1964.

62. Gowda, Anniah, H.H., "Contemporary Creative Writers in English in India", *The Literary Half-Yearly*, Vol. X, No. 1, Jan. 1969.

63. Gowda, Anniah, H.H., "Mulk Raj Anand", *The Literary Half-Yearly*, Vol. VI, No. 1, Jan. 1965.

64. Gowda, Anniah, H.H., "Review of Saros Cowasjee's So Many Freedoms and Coolie : An Assessment", *The Literary Half-Yearly*, Vol. XIX, No. 2, July 1978.

65. Gupta, Balarama, G.S., "Anand's Big Heart : A Study", *The Banasthali Patrika*, Year 5, No. 13, July 1969.

66. Gupta, Balarama, G.S., "Anand's Old Woman and the Cow in Humanist Perspective", *Karnatak University Journal — Humanities*, Vol. XIV, 1970.

67. Gupta, Balarama, G.S., "Coolie — A Prose Epic of Modern India", *Karnatak University Journal — Humanities*, Vol. XII, 1968.

68. Gupta, Balarama, G.S., "The Humanism of Dr. Mulk Raj Anand", *Contemporary Indian Literature*, Vol. VII, 1967.

69. Gupta, Balarama, G.S., "Projecting Indian Literary Image", *Littcrit*, Vol. II, No. 1, June 1976.

70. Gupta, Balarama, G.S., "Review of Mulk Raj Anand's Morning Face", *The Karnatak University Journal — Humanities*, Vol. XIII, 1969.

71. Gupta, Balarama, G.S., "Review of M.K. Naik's Mulk Raj Anand", *Indian Literature*, Vol. XVI, Nos. 3 & 4, July-Dec. 1973.

72. Gupta, Balarama, G.S., "Some Reflections on Indian Writing in English", *The Journal of Indian Writing in English*, Vol. I, No. 2, July 1973.

73. Gupta, Balarama, G.S., "Towards a Closer Understanding of Anand", *Indo-English Literature : A Collection of Critical Essays* (Ed.) K.K. Sharma, Ghaziabad : Vimal Prakashan, 1971.

74. Gupta, Balarama, G.S., "Woman in Anand's Shorter Fiction", *The Karnatak University Journal — Humanities*, Vol. XIII, 1969.

75. Gupta, L.N., "Review of Confession of a Lover", *The Sunday Hitwada*, 7 March 1976.

76. G.S. Balarama Gupta, "Anand in Letters", *Kakatiya Journal of English Studies*, Vol. II, No. I, Spring, 1977, Department of English, Kakatiya University, Warangal.

77. Henderson, Philip, "Mulk Raj Anand", *The Novel Today*, London : The Bodley Head, 1936.

78. Henderson, Philip, "Indian Literature of the Past Fifty Years 1917-1967" (Ed.) C.D. Narasimhaiah, Mysore : University of Mysore, 1970.

79. Henderson, Philip, "Indian Literature Since Independence : A Symposium" (Ed.) K.R. Srinivasa Iyengar, Delhi : Sahitya Akadami, 1973.

80. Hilla Vakeel, "Three Views on Coolie", *Kakatiya Journal of English Studies*, Vol. II, No. 1, Spring 1977, Mulk Raj Anand Special Number, Department of English, Kakatiya University, Warangal.

81. *Hindustan Standard*, "Fiction : Autobiography", 14 Sept. 1969.

82. Iyengar, Shrinivasa, K.R., "A General Survey", *The Novel in Modern India* (Ed.) Iqbal Bakhtiyar, Bombay : The P.E.N. All India Centre, 1964.

83. Iyengar, Shrinivasa, K.R., "Indo-Anglian Literature", Bombay : The P.E.N. All-India Centre, 1943.

84. Iyengar, Shrinivasa, K.R., "Review of Mulk Raj Anand's Confession of a Lover", *The Journal of Indian Writing in English*, Vol. IV, No. 2, July 1976.

85. Iyengar, Shrinivasa, K.R., "We belong to Suffering...!", Review of Mulk Raj Anand's Coolie, *Deccan Herald*, 5 Nov. 1972.

86. Joshi, K.N. and B. Shyamala Rao, "Studies in Indo-Anglian Literature", Bareilly : Prakash Book Depot, N.D.

87. Jack Lindsay, "Mulk Raj Anand", *Kakatiya Journal of English Studies*, Vol. II, No. I, Spring 1977, Mulk Raj Anand Special Number, Department of English, Kakatiya University, Warangal.

88. Kantak, V.Y., "The Language of Indian Fiction in English", *Critical Essays on Indian Writing in English* (Ed.) M.K. Naik *et al.*, Madras : The Macmillan Company of India Ltd., 1972.

89. Karanth, K.A., "How Deep is Western Influence on Indian Writers of Fiction?", *Literary Criterion*, Vol. VII, No. 2, Summer 1966.

90. Kaushik, R.K., *Indo-English Literature : A Collection of Critical Essays* (Ed.) K.K. Sharma, Ghaziabad : Vimal Prakashan, 1977.

91. Kaul, J.L., "Contemporary Trends in Indian Writing", *The Indian P.E.N.*, Vol. XXVI, No. 7, July 1960.

92. Kurmanadham, K., "The Novels of Dr. Mulk Raj Anand", *Triveni*, Vol. XXXVI, No. 3, October 1967.

93. Kurmanadham, K., "Women characters in Dr. Anand's novels", *Contemporary Indian Literature*, Vol. VI, June-July 1966.

94. Kushwaha, M.S., "A Neglected area of Indo-Anglian Writing", *The Journal of Indian Writing in English*, Vol. VI, No. 1, Jan. 1978.

95. Kaushik, R.K., 'Indian Princes Again', *The Literary Half-Yearly*, Vol. 12, No. 1, January 1971.

96. K.V.S. Murti, "Seven Summers", Anand's Fictional Matrix, *Kakatiya Journal of English Studies*, Vol. II, No. 1, Spring 1977, Mulk Raj Anand Special Number, Department of English, Kakatiya University, Warangal.

97. Lal, P., "The Concept of an Indian Literature", Six Essays, Calcutta : Writers Workshop, 1968.

98. *Left Review*, "Manifesto of the Indian Progressive Writers' Association, London", Vol. 2, No. 5, February 1936.

99. *Link*, "Plight of Harijan, Today", 2 February 1969.

100. Marath, S. Menon, "The Indian Novelists", *Life and Letters*, Vol. 59, December 1948.

101. Menon, K.P.S., "It is the Morning Sun", *Sunday Tribune*, 19 October 1959.

102. Mukherjee, Meenakshi, "The Tractor and the Plough : The Contrasted Vision of Sudhin Ghose and Mulk Raj Anand", *Indian Literature*, Vol. 13, No. 1, 1970.

103. Malik, Keshav, "The Indian Writers' Problems", *ACLALS Bulletin*, Fourth Series No. 2, 1975.

104. Mathur, D.P., "Mulk Raj Anand's Untouchable and Richard Wright's Bigger Thomas : A Comparatives Study in Social Protest and Affirmation", *The Literary Half-Yearly*, Vol. XIX, No. 2, July 1978.

105. Misra, Gopalachandra, "Indian Writer and his Problems", *Contemporary Indian Literature*, Vol. XII, April-June 1972.

106. Mokashi-Punekar, S., "The Indo-Anglian Creed", Calcutta : Writers Workshop, 1972.

107. Mukherjee, Meenakshi, "Awareness of Audience in Indo-Anglian Fiction", *Quest*, LII, Jan.-March 1967.

108. Mukherjee, Meenakshi, "Beyond the Village, An Aspect of Mulk Raj Anand", *Critical Essays on Indian Writing in English*, (Ed.) M.K. Naik *et al.*, Madras : The Macmillan Co. of India Ltd., 1977.

109. Mukherjee, Meenakshi, "Style in Indo-Anglian Fiction", *Indian Writing Today*, Vol. IV, No. 11, Jan.-March 1970.

110. Mukherjee, Meenakshi, "The Tractor and the Plough : The Contrasted Visions of Sudhin Ghose and Mulk Raj Anand", *Indian Literature*, Vol. XIII, No. 1, 1970.

111. Mukherjee, Meenakshi, *The Twice Born Fiction*, Delhi : Arnold-Heinemann, 1974.

112. Mukherjee, Sujit, "The Indo-Anglian Novelist as Best Seller", *Literature East and West*, Vol. XIII, Nos. 1-2, 1969.

113. Mukherjee, Sujit, "The Indo-English Literature — An Essay in Definition", *Critical Essays on Indian Writing in English* (Ed.) M.K. Naik *et al.*, Madras : The Macmillan Co. of India Ltd., 1972.

114. Murti, Suryanarayana, K.V., "The Motif of Virtue in Dr. Mulk Raj Anand's Novels", *Contemporary Indian Literature*, Vol. V, No. 1, Jan. 1966.

115. Murti, Suryanarayana, K.V., "Review of Perspectives on Mulk Raj Anand (Ed.) K. Sharma, *The Journal of Indian Writing in English*, Vol. VII, No. 2, July 1979.

116. Murti, Suryanarayana, K.V. ,"The Theme of Salvation : Treatment by Mulk Raj Anand and R.K. Narayan", *Triveni*, Vol. XXXIV, No. 3, October 1965.

117. Marlene Fisher, 'Confession of a Lover', *Kakatiya Journal of English Studies*, Vol. II, No. 1, Spring, 1977, Mulk Raj Anand Special Number, Department of English, Kakatiya University, Warangal, India.

118. *New Stateman*, "The Tea-Garden Coolie", Vol. 14, No. 332, 3 July 1937.

119. Niven, Alastair, "A Modern Indian Intellect", *The Journal of Commonwalth Literature*, Vol. 6, No. 1, June 1971.

120. Niven, Alastair, "The Lalu Trilogy of Mulk Raj Anand", *The Literary Half-Yearly*, Vol. 13, No. 1, January 1972.

121. Naik, M.K., "In Defence of Indian Writing in English", *Indo-English Literature : A Collection of Critical Essays* (Ed.) K.K. Sharma, Ghaziabad : Vimal Prakashan, 1977.

122. Naik, M.K., "The Achievement of Mulk Raj Anand", *The Journal of Indian Writing in English*, Vol. I, No. 1, 1973.

123. Naik, M.K., "Gandhiji and Indian Writing in English", *Critical Essays on Indian Writing in English* (Ed.) M.K. Naik *et al.*, Madras : The Macmillan Co. of India Ltd., 1972.

124. Naiker, Basavaraj, S., "Review of Kakatiya Journal of English Studies", Mulk Raj Anand Special Number, *The Journal of Indian Writing in English*, Vol. V, No. 2, July 1977.

125. Nanda Kumar, Prema, "Achievement of the Indo-Anglian Novelist", *The Literary Criterion*, Vol. V, No. 1, Winter, 1961.

126. Nanda Kumar, Prema, "English : A Piquant Effect", *Indian Literature*, Vol. IX, No. 4, 1966.

127. Narasimhaiah, C.D., *Moving Frontiers of English Studies in India*, Delhi : S. Chand Co., 1977.

128. Narasimhaiah, C.D., *The Swan and the Eagle*, Simla : Indian Institute of Advanced Study, 1969.

129. Narasimhan, Raji, "Sensibility under Stress : Aspects of Indo-English Fiction", New Delhi : Ashajanak Prakashan, 1976.

130. Narayan, Shyamala, A., "Indian English Novel : Steady Growth", *Littcrit*, Vol. V, No. 2, Dec. 1979.

131. N.G.M., "Review of the Old Woman and the Cow", *The Indian P.E.N.*, Vol. XXVII, No. 6, June 1961.

132. Nicholson, Kai, "A Presentation of Social Problems in the Indo-Anglian and the Anglo-Indian Novel", Bombay : Jaico Publications, 1972.

133. Niranjan, Shiva, "The Nature and Extent of Gandhi's Impact on the Early Novels of Mulk Raj Anand and Raja Rao", *Commonwealth Quarterly*, Vol. III, No. II, June 1979.

134. Niven, Alastair, "The Lalu Trilogy of Mulk Raj Anand", *Readings in Commonwealth Literature* (Ed.) William Walsh, Oxford : Clarendon Press, 1973.

135. Niven, Alastair, "Myth into Moral : Mulk Raj Anand's The Old Woman and the Cow", *ACLALS Bulletin*, Fourth Series, No. 3, 1975.

136. Pachori, Satya, S., "Anand's Untouchable : Bakha's Journey to a Sense of Selfhood", MLA Session on South Asian Literature, Utah: East-West Centre, 1976.

137. Pandia, M.A., "Indo-Anglian Fiction Since Independence", *Triveni*, Vol. XXVII, No. 3, Oct. 1956.

138. Pandit, Manorama, "Review of Mulk Raj Anand's The Road", *World Literature Written in English*, Vol. XIV, No. 2, Nov. 1975.

139. Pant, M.C., "Mulk Raj Anand — The Man", *Contemporary Indian Literature*, V, 11-12, Nov.-Dec. 1965.

140. Parameswaran, Uma, *A Study of Representative Indo-English Novelists*, Bombay : Vikas Publishing House, 1976.

141. Pillai, Takazhi Sivasankara, "Indian Literature and the Contemporary Scene", *Contemporary Indian Literature*, Vol. XII, April-June, 1972.

142. Prasad, Illa, "Indian English-Literary Hangover from Colonial Days", *CIEFL, News letter*, Vol. XIV, No. 1, Jan. 1978.

143. Radhakrishnan, N., "The Image of Gandhi in Indo-Anglian Novels", *Research and Criticism* (Ed.), Radhakrishanan, Annamalai, Research Scholars' Association, 1975.

144. Raghavacharyulu, D.V.K., "Commonwalth Literature : Metaphors of Identity", *ACLALS Bulletin*, Fourth Series, No. 2, 1975.

145. Raghavacharyulu, D.V.K., "The Critical Response", Madras : The Macmillan Co. of India Ltd., 1980.

146. Raghavacharyulu, D.V.K., "The Task Ahead — The Problem of a Literary History for Indian Writing in English," *Critical Essays on Indian Writing in English* (Ed.) M.K. Naik *et al.*, Madras : The Macmillan Co. of India Ltd., 1972.

147. Rajan, B., "Remarks on Identity and Nationality", *Literature East and West*, Vol. IX, No. 2, 1965, 91-94.

148. Ramakrishna, D., "Academics and Yogis : Reflections on the Recent Indo-English Fiction," *The Journal of Indian Writing in English*, Vol. VII, No. 2, July 1979.

149. Ramamurthy, K.S., "The Puranic Tradition and Modern

Indo-Anglian Fiction", *Indian Writing Today*, Vol. VI, No. 11, Jan-March, 1970.

150. Ramamurthy, K.S., "The Rise of the Novel in India and the Rise of English Novel", *English and India* (Ed.) M. Manuel and K. Ayyappa Paniker, Madras : The Macmillian Co. of India Ltd., 1978.

151. Rao, Chalapati, M., "The Indo-Anglian", *The Illustrated Weekly of India*, 26 May 1963.

152. Rao, Damodar, Afterword to Mulk Raj Anand", *Untouchable*, Mysore : Geetha Book House, 1978.

153. Rao, Raghavendra, P., "Mulk Raj Anand", *The Twofold Voice : Essay on Indian Writing in English* (Ed.) D.V.K. Raghavacharyulu, Guntur : Navodaya Publishers, 1971.

154. Rao, Subba, T.V.," Indian Writing in English : Is there are work in it?", Madurai : Koodal Publishers, 1976.

155. Reddy, Venkata, K., "Anand's A Master of Arts", *The Journal of Indian Writing in English*, Vol. V, No. 2, July 1977.

156. Rao, Vinod, "Feudal Caste, Terror on Hapless Harijans", *Blitz*, 16th December 1972.

157. R.T. Robertson, "Untouchable as an archetypal novel", *Kakatiya Journal of English Studies*, Vol. II, No. 1, Spring 1977, Mulk Raj Anand Special Number, Department of English, Kakatiya University, Warangal, India.

158. Sharma, G.P., "Nationalism in Indo-Anglian Fiction", Delhi : Sterling Publishers Pvt. Ltd., 1978.

159. Shahane, Vasant, A., "Ando-Anglian Fiction and the Question of Form", *The Journal of Indian Writing in English*, Vol. II, No. 2, July 1974.

160. Sharma, Atma Ram, "Review of Alastair Niven's The Yoke of Pity", *The Journal of Indian Writing in English*, Vol. VII, No. 2, July 1979.

161. Singh, Narenderpal, "The Indian Novel : Its Present and Future", *The Indian P.E.N.*, Vol. XXXXIII, Nos. 7-8, July-Aug. 1973.

162. Singh, R.S., "From Resentment to Social Protest, Mulk Raj Anand", *Indian Novel in English*, New Delhi : Arnold-Heinemann, 1977.

163. Spencer, Dorothy, M., "Indian Fiction in English — An Annotated Bibliography", Philadelphia : Univ. of Pennsylvania Press, 1960.

164. Srivastava, Kamatacharan, "Indian Writing in English, Some Reflections", *Indian Writing in English* (Ed.) K.N. Sinha, Delhi : Heritage Publishers, 1979.

165. Steinvorth, Klaus, *The Indo-English Novel*, Wieshbanden : Franz Steiner Verlag, 1975.

166. Sundaram, P.S., "Indo-Anglian Literature", *Eve's Weekly*, 13-19 Aug, 1977.

167. S. Laxmana Murthy, "Bakha : An Existential Analysis", *Kakatiya Journal of English Studies*, Vol. II, No. 1, Spring, 1977, Mulk Raj Anand Special Number, Department of English, Kakatiya University, Warangal, India.

168. Sanjay Bhatt, "The Lost Child", *Kakatiya Journal of English Studies*, Vol. II, No. 1, Spring 1977, Mulk Raj Anand Special Number, Department of English, Kakatiya University, Warangal, India.

169. Suresh Kohli, "The Road", *Kakatiya Journal of English Studies*, Vol. II, No. 1, Spring 1977, Mulk Raj Anand Special Number, Department of English, Kakatiya University, Warangal, India.

Index